THE GREAT GATSBY

Retold by **Gina D. B. Clemen**

Activities by **Louis Vaughan**

Illustrated by **Anna and Elena Balbusso**

Editor: Robert Hill
Design and art direction: Nadia Maestri
Computer graphics: Sara Blasigh
Picture research: Laura Lagomarsino

Picture credits: Department of Rare Books and Special Collections,
Princeton University Library: 5; © Bettmann / CORBIS: 9; Library of
Congress Prints and Photographs Division, Washington: 69, 124; Yale
Collection of American Americana, Beinecke Rare Book and
Manuscript Library: 123.

DEALINK, DEAFLIX are trademarks licensed by De Agostini SpA

We would be happy to receive your comments and suggestions, and
give you any other information concerning our material.
info@blackcat-cideb.com
blackcat-cideb.com

CISQ CISQ CERT
TEXTBOOKS AND
TEACHING MATERIALS
The quality of the publisher's
design, production and sales processes has been
certified to the standard of
UNI EN ISO 9001

Printed in Italy by Italgrafica, Novara

CONTENTS

START
END
These symbols indicate the beginning and end of the passages linked to the reading activities.

A Note on the Author
and his Times

Youth

Francis Scott Key Fitzgerald was born on September 24, 1896 in St. Paul, Minnesota. Not only was he one of America's major writers, but he was also a social historian who gave the name to the Jazz Age. Jazz became very popular in the 1920s with great musicians such as Louis Armstrong and Benny Goodman and with the invention of the phonograph record.

Fitzgerald's fiction is a rich, detailed and realistic account of American life in the 1920s. His ambition, self-confidence and passion created a writer whose intricate personal life often resembled a work of fiction. Most of his life was a struggle [1] between the temptation of a glamorous [2] and wealthy social life, and a strong desire to write.

Fitzgerald attended Princeton University but did not graduate because he often neglected his studies and spent most of his time on the football team and the social life of the university. He was an active member of the Triangle Club, which produced original university plays. Already as a university student Fitzgerald was attracted by the best things that life could offer.

In 1917 he left Princeton and joined the U.S. Army as a second lieutenant, but he never fought in the First World War. During his

---

1. **struggle** : battle, fight.
2. **glamorous** : elegant, attractive.

F. Scott Fitzgerald photographed in 1920,
at the very beginning of the Jazz Age.

military training he began writing his first novel, *This Side of Paradise*. His army career took him to Camp Sheridan, near Montgomery, Alabama, where he met and fell deeply in love with Zelda Sayre, a rich girl from the South. Their relationship was not easy from the beginning. They were both quite independent individuals and they both wanted social and financial success in their lives. Zelda often wondered if Fitzgerald would ever make enough money to marry her! This made a strong impression on Fitzgerald and influenced the importance he gave to money and social connections throughout his life. In fact, she married him in April 1920 only after the publication of *This Side of Paradise*. The couple went to live in New York.

Success

Fitzgerald's first novel was immediately successful but it was not considered a very good book, although it revealed how many young people of the 1920s lived. With his good looks, popularity and social know-how, he was a sort of model for upper-class American youth. World War I had just finished and America wanted to have fun. For those who could afford it, like the Fitzgeralds, parties and drinking became a way of life. All over New York City people telephoned each other planning parties.

For a while the Fitzgeralds were successful and happy as they went from one party to the next. But their expensive, superficial lifestyle [1] did not give them any kind of the security or stability which they both needed.

---

1. **lifestyle** : the way in which you live.

Although Fitzgerald earned a great amount of money, he began his lifelong practice of borrowing from his agent and his publisher. He had no control over his extravagant spending habits or Zelda's. He didn't really care enough about money—he only cared about the lifestyle money could bring. In *The Great Gatsby* Fitzgerald sympathizes with [1] Jay Gatsby, a tremendously successful but illegal businessman, despised by the more established wealthy families. Gatsby is the living example of the "American Dream": a nobody from nowhere who achieves immense wealth with his own capacities. Nick Carraway says to him towards the end of the novel, "You're worth the whole bunch [2] of them." It is interesting to note that both the author and his main character, Jay Gatsby, became victims of their dreams.

On October 26, 1921 Fitzgerald and Zelda's child, Frances, was born, but she was a burden [3] for Zelda. Fitzgerald's second novel, *The Beautiful and the Damned*, was published in 1922 but it was not very well received. It was considered a serious book, perhaps too serious. One of its major defects was the conflict between Fitzgerald's natural feelings and the fashionable attitudes of the pessimistic intellectuals of his time. In the novel he tried to show the meaning of the life he and Zelda had been living. But he was not able to create two protagonists who were beautiful and damned. Instead they were pitiful and silly.

Their grandiose lifestyle in New York became extremely costly and Fitzgerald worked for important magazines, such as the

---

1. **sympathizes with** : (here) shows approval, agrees with.
2. **bunch** : group.
3. **burden** : a heavy responsibility, a big problem.

Saturday Evening Post, to earn more money. But he and Zelda were always deeply in debt. They had heard that life in Europe was very cheap and so they moved to France, where they hoped to find a new balance in their lives. However, there was more trouble ahead of them.

Europe

Zelda met a handsome French aviator and they fell in love. When Fitzgerald discovered what was happening, his reaction was very violent and the love affair was soon over. In Paris Fitzgerald met other important American writers such as Ernest Hemingway and Gertrude Stein.

Early in November 1924 the Fitzgeralds decided to spend the winter in Rome. They hated Rome because no one knew who they were. They started drinking heavily again and they quarreled [1] a lot. Fitzgerald got into a fight with a taxi driver and was badly beaten up. [2] From Rome they went to Capri and then back to France.

The Great Gatsby was published in April 1925 and it represented the high point in Fitzgerald's literary career. He was able to understand and portray the decadence, hypocrisy and materialism of the Jazz Age better than any other writer of his period. However, the initial sales of *The Great Gatsby*, about 20,000 copies, were a big disappointment for Fitzgerald. There never seemed to be enough money for him and Zelda, and their lives of constant partying and drinking had become a nightmare.

1. **quarreled** : had disagreements.
2. **beaten up** : hit violently.

Scott, Zelda and their daughter Scottie photographed somewhere in Italy on one of their visits to Europe after the publication of *The Great Gatsby*.

The summer of 1925 in Paris was in Fitzgerald's words, "one of 1,000 parties and no work". In August they went to Antibes in the south of France and continued partying with many socially important people. They decided to return to the United States to start working seriously at the end of 1925. But Hollywood, where Fitzgerald was working as a scriptwriter [1] for United Artists, was

---

1. **scriptwriter** : a person who writes the stories for films.

another continuous party where people played grotesque jokes on each other. At one party Fitzgerald took the watches and jewelry of the guests and boiled them in a saucepan of tomato soup!

Zelda's Breakdown [1]

Once again the couple attempted to put order and meaning into their lives and moved back to the East Coast in 1927. Their marriage was deteriorating, but Fitzgerald was finally able to do some work on his novel *Tender is the Night*.

As a young girl Zelda wanted to be a ballet dancer and at the age of twenty-eight she decided to start studying ballet dancing again. She and Fitzgerald spent the summer of 1928 in Paris, where she took ballet lessons. Ballet had become an obsession for Zelda.

On their return to the United States in September they were bankrupt. In 1930 Zelda suffered her first serious nervous breakdown. Fitzgerald loved his wife and he felt her suffering deeply. He also knew that one of the causes of her problems was his heavy drinking. This intensified his remorse and compassion.

In 1933 Fitzgerald finally completed *Tender is the Night*, in spite of his alcoholism and his wife's mental illness. Zelda had her third severe breakdown in 1934 and for the rest of her life she was never well again. Although she returned home occasionally, she spent most of her life in a mental hospital. Fitzgerald was desperate, in severe financial difficulty, and he drank heavily.

---

1. **breakdown** : an unnatural condition of deep anxiety, worrying, crying and depression that sometimes leads to mental illness.

Decline

Taps at Reveille, a collection of short stories, was published in the spring of 1935. These were terribly difficult years for the writer, because the quality of his work declined and he was not able to control his drinking.

In July 1937 he went to Hollywood to work as a scriptwriter again. Here he met Sheila Graham, a famous Hollywood journalist, and fell in love with her. This was a lucky meeting for Fitzgerald because at this point in his life he needed a woman to look after and worry about.

However, he was not very successful as a scriptwriter and by 1939 he was discouraged because he could not find work. He wrote the first part of his last novel, *The Last Tycoon,* sitting in bed because he was very weak. On December 21, 1940, after a second, severe heart attack, Fitzgerald died. His last novel, although unfinished, was published in 1941.

Few people came to his funeral in Hollywood—in some ways it was similar to Jay Gatsby's. Zelda died in 1948 during a fire in the mental hospital and was buried beside him.

Answer the following questions.

1   Why can F. Scott Fitzgerald also be considered a social historian?
....

2   Why didn't Fitzgerald graduate from university?
....

3   What things were important to Zelda Sayre?
....

4   What happened to wealthy young Americans after World War I?
....

5   What were the problems with *The Beautiful and The Damned*?
....

6   Why did Fitzgerald want to make a lot of money?
....

7   Why did the Fitzgeralds move to Europe?
....

8   What personal problems did they face in Europe?
....

9   What were the Fitzgeralds' favorite social activities?
....

10   What was Fitzgerald's job in Hollywood?
....

11   What was one of the causes of Zelda's emotional breakdowns?
....

12   Describe Fitzgerald's last years.
....

2 Discussion
Is there a writer in your culture who is similar to F. Scott Fitzgerald?

Before you read

1 Nick's background

Read the first part of Chapter One. For questions 1-12 complete the sentences.

1 Nick's father told him not to criticize anyone because ....

....

2 Nick grew up in ....

3 Nick's family had been important for ....

4 Nick graduated from New Haven University in ....

5 Nick felt restless in the United States because ....

....

6 Nick went East to learn ....

7 Instead of finding rooms in New York City, Nick rented ....

....

8 To live in his small and ugly house Nick paid ....

9 East Egg and West Egg were ....

10 Mr Gatsby's home was an imitation of a ....

11 Daisy was Nick's ....

12 Nick had known Tom in ....

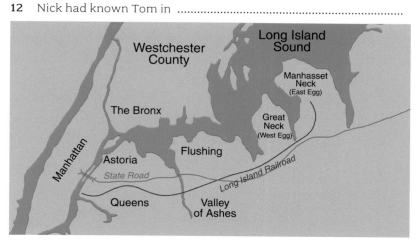

Part of **New York** state. To the east of Manhattan and to the south of Westchester County you can see here the north-western part of **Long Island**, where the story is set.

START

When I was younger my father gave me some advice that I've been thinking about ever since.

"Whenever you feel like criticizing anyone," he told me, "just remember that all the people in the world haven't had the advantages that you've had."

After spending some time in New York I came back to this Midwestern [1] city where I grew up. My family have been important, well-to-do [2] people for three generations. My grandfather's brother came here in 1851 and started the business that my father works in today.

I graduated from New Haven University [3] in 1915 and then took part in the First World War. I enjoyed Europe so much that I came back feeling restless. [4] So I decided to go East and learn the bond business. [5] Everybody I knew was in the bond business. Father agreed to pay for my living costs for a year and in 1922 I came East, permanently, I thought.

I intended to find rooms in New York City, but when a young man at the office suggested that we rent a house together in the country, it sounded like a great idea. He found a small house

---

1. **midwestern** : part of the Midwest, the central pasrt of the US east of the Rocky Mountains.
2. **well-to-do** : upper middle-class.
3. **New Haven University** : today this university is known as Yale University.
4. **restless** : always moving, unable to stay still.
5. **bond business** : the buying and selling of certificates of debt.

to rent at eighty dollars a month, but at the last minute his company sent him to Washington and I went to the country alone. I had a Finnish woman who made my bed and cooked breakfast.

And so with the sunshine and the abundant green leaves growing on the trees, I had the feeling that life was beginning again with the summer.

There was so much to read and I bought a lot of books about banking and investments, which stood on my shelf promising to reveal the secrets of wealth.

By chance I had rented a house in one of the strangest communities in North America. It was on Long Island, [1] which stretches more than sixty miles east of New York City.

On Long Island there are two unusual formations of land that look almost like two eggs and are separated by a bay.

I lived at West Egg, the less fashionable of the two. My house was between two huge houses, near the sea. The one on my right was colossal. It was an imitation of a French palace with a tower on one side, a splendid swimming pool and beautiful lawns [2] and gardens. It was Mr Gatsby's home. My house was ugly and small, but I had a view of the water, of part of my neighbor's lawn and I lived near millionaires, all for eighty dollars a month.

Across the bay the white palaces of the fashionable East Egg shone on the water. The history of the summer really begins on the day I went to have dinner with Tom and Daisy Buchanan. Daisy was my second cousin and I had known Tom in college.

---

1. **Long Island** : see map on page 13.
2. **lawns** : areas of cut grass in a garden or park.

THE GREAT GATSBY

Tom was one of the most powerful football players New Haven University had ever had. His family was extremely wealthy. Now he had left Chicago and had come East, bringing his own polo horses with him. It was hard to imagine that a man of my own age was so rich.

I don't know why they came East. They had spent a year in France for no particular reason and then drifted [1] here and there, wherever people played polo and were rich.

On the telephone Daisy said they were going to stay, but I didn't believe it. Tom would drift on forever looking for excitement.

And so it happened that on a warm and windy evening I drove over to East Egg to see two old friends I hardly knew. Their house was even more elaborate than I had expected—a red and white colonial mansion, [2] looking over the bay. Tom Buchanan was standing with his legs apart on the front porch. [3]

He was a robust man of thirty, with a rather hard mouth and an arrogant manner. His body was powerful—it was a cruel body.

His rough [4] speaking voice added to the impression of a bad-tempered individual. There were men at New Haven who really hated him. We had never been close friends, but I had the feeling that he approved of me and wanted me to like him. We talked for a few minutes on the sunny porch.

"I've got a nice place here," he said, his eyes moving about restlessly. "It belonged to Demaine, the oil man. Let's go inside."

1. **drifted** : moved about without a reason or purpose.
2. **mansion** : a large, expensive house with land around it.
3. **porch** : covered area at the entrance (see picture on page 17).
4. **rough** : harsh, unpleasant.

We walked through a high hallway into a bright rosy-colored room with open French windows at each end. A breeze [1] blew through the room blowing the curtains like pale flags.

In the room there was an enormous couch [2] on which two young women, both dressed in white, were lying.

The younger of the two was a stranger to me and did not move at all when I came in.

The other girl, Daisy, made an attempt to rise and then she laughed an absurd, charming little laugh. I laughed too and came forward into the room.

"I'm so, so happy to see you." She laughed again and held my hand. She said in a soft voice that the name of the other woman was Baker.

Miss Baker's lips moved a little and she bent [3] her head very slightly in my direction.

My cousin started asking me questions in her low, exciting voice. Her face was sad and lovely, with bright eyes and a passionate mouth, but it was the excitement in her voice that men found difficult to forget.

"Oh, Nick, you should see the baby."

"I'd like to."

"She's asleep. She's two years old. Have you seen her?"

"Never."

Tom Buchanan, who had been moving around the room restlessly, put his hand on my shoulder.

"What are you doing, Nick?"

---

1. **breeze** : a light wind.
2. **couch** :
3. **bent** : leaned.

"I sell bonds."

"Who do you work for?"

I told him.

"Never heard of them," he said firmly.

This annoyed me. "You will hear of them," I said.

At this point Miss Baker suddenly came to life and stood up.

"I'm stiff," [1] she complained. "I've been lying on the couch too long."

I enjoyed looking at her. She was a slender [2] girl with gray eyes and a charming, dissatisfied face. I realized that I had seen her, or her picture, somewhere before.

"You live in West Egg. I know somebody there," she said.

"I don't know a single—"

"You must know Gatsby."

"Gatsby?" demanded Daisy. "What Gatsby?"

Before I could say that he was my neighbor, the butler [3] announced dinner and Tom put his hand under my arm and moved me from the room.

We followed the two young women onto a rosy-colored porch where a table was set for dinner.

---

1. **stiff** : rigid, have difficulty moving.

2. **slender** : thin and graceful.
3. **butler** : a male servant.

Miss Baker and Daisy talked together in a manner that was as cool as their white dresses. They were here and they accepted Tom and me, making only a polite effort to entertain or be entertained.

"You make me feel uncivilized, Daisy," I said. "Can't you talk about agriculture or something?"

My comment had a strange effect on Tom.

"Civilization is going to pieces!" he said violently. "Have you read *The Rise of Colored Empires* by Goddard?"

"Why, no," I answered, rather surprised.

"Well, it's a fine book and everybody ought to read it. It says that if we aren't careful the white race will be pushed under by the colored races. It's all very scientific."

"Tom's getting very profound," said Daisy. "He reads deep books with long words in them."

"These books are all scientific. Our race has produced all the things that make up civilization—art, science and all that. If we're not careful these other races will control things."

The telephone rang inside the house and the butler went to answer it. He came back, whispered something in Tom's ear and without a word Tom went inside.

Daisy looked at me and said, "I love to see you at my table, Nick. You remind me of a—of a rose."

This was not true. She was saying the first thing that came into her head, but her warm voice was exciting. Then suddenly she excused herself and went into the house.

Miss Baker and I looked at each other. I wanted to speak when she sat up and said, "Ssh! Don't talk. I want to hear what Tom is saying on the telephone."

"Is something happening?" I asked.

"You don't know?" said Miss Baker. "I thought everybody knew. Tom's got a woman in New York."

"He's got a woman?" I repeated stupidly.

"Yes. She shouldn't telephone him at dinner, though."

Tom and Daisy came back to the table and I avoided looking at their eyes.

After a few minutes we got up from the table and Tom and Miss Baker went inside. I followed Daisy to the front porch where we sat and talked for a while.

"Nick, do you know what I said when my daughter was born?"

"Tell me."

"I said, 'I'm glad it's a girl and I hope she'll be a beautiful little fool [1]—that's the best thing a girl can be in this world.'"

Tom and Miss Baker sat on a long couch in the rose-red room and she read out loud to him from the *Saturday Evening Post*. [2] When Daisy and I came in she stopped reading and stood up.

"Ten o'clock," she said. "Time for me to go to bed."

"Jordan's playing in a match tomorrow," explained Daisy.

"Oh—you're *Jordan* Baker," I said.

Now I knew why her face was familiar. She was a well-known golf player. Her face had looked out at me from many photographs of her sports life. I had heard a story about her too, a critical, unpleasant story that I had forgotten.

"Good night," she said. "Good night, Mr Carraway. See you soon." She went up the stairs.

1. **fool** : idiot.
2. *Saturday Evening Post* : a popular American magazine.

"Of course you will," said Daisy. "Come over often, Nick, and I think I'll arrange a marriage!"

"She's a nice girl," said Tom.

"Is she from New York?" I asked.

"She's from Louisville, my home town. We grew up together," said Daisy.

A few minutes later I got up to go home. Tom and Daisy came to the door with me and stood side by side in a cheerful square of light.

I was confused and a little disgusted as I drove away. It seemed to me that the thing for Daisy to do was to run out of the house with her child in her arms. As for Tom, the fact that "he had a woman in New York" was less surprising than the fact that he had been upset [1] by a book.

When I got home to West Egg, it was a bright, moonlit night. Twenty yards [2] away, in my neighbor's mansion, a man was standing with his hands in his pockets looking up at the stars. Something in the way he stood suggested that he was Mr Gatsby himself. He stretched out his arms towards the dark water and I think he was trembling. [3] I looked at the sea too, but all I could see was a small, green light on the coast of East Egg.

1. **upset** : worried, anxious, troubled.
2. **yards** : measurement of length (1 yard=0.91 meters).
3. **trembling** : shaking.

The text and **beyond**

1 Comprehension check

Answer the following questions.

1 What kind of life did Tom and Daisy lead before coming to Long Island?
2 What do you know about Nick? What do you know about Tom?
3 What kind of relationship do Tom and Nick have?
4 Who is Miss Baker?
5 Who does Miss Baker know in West Egg?
6 How does Tom react when Nick says the word "uncivilized"?
7 Who calls Tom on the telephone?
8 Why does Miss Baker object to the phone call that Tom receives?
9 Why is Miss Baker's face familiar to Nick?
10 How does Nick feel when he leaves Tom and Daisy's house?

FCE 2 The young and the restless

You are a newspaper reporter who has visited Tom and Daisy at their home. Write a short article about what you saw and heard, but also what you think of these rich young people.

Include in your article a brief description of:

*   the house
*   Tom, Daisy and Miss Baker
*   Tom and Daisy's lifestyle before returning to America
*   how they talk and what they talk about

Conclude your article by saying what impression these people made on you during your short visit. Write between 120-180 words.

You can begin your article like this:

A Visit to an East Egg Mansion

For our series of articles "The Young and the Restless" we visited the exclusive home of Mr and Mrs Tom Buchanan in fashionable East Egg, Long Island. Their house, which once belonged to...

FCE ③ Sentence transformation

Complete the second sentence so that it has a similar meaning to the
first sentence, using the word given. <u>Do not change the word given</u>.
You must use between two and five words, including the word given.
There is an example at the beginning (0).

0 I enjoyed Europe so much that I came back feeling restless.
   had
   I came back feeling restless ..... *because I had enjoyed Europe* ..... so
   much.

1 Father agreed to pay for my living costs.
   would
   Father .... for my living costs.

2 A young man at the office suggested that we rent a house together
   in the country.
   why
   A young man at the office said, "..................................... a
   house together in the country?"

3 On the telephone Daisy said they were going to stay.
   are
   On the telephone Daisy said, "............................... stay."

4 I drove over to East Egg to see two old friends I hardly knew.
   not
   I drove over to East Egg to see two old friends .... well.

5 My cousin started asking me questions.
   ask
   My cousin .... questions.

6 Tom said, "The white race will be pushed under by the colored
   races."
   push
   Tom told us .... the white race under.

7 I had heard a story about her that I had forgotten.
   remembered
   I .... that I had heard.

8 It seemed to me that the thing for Daisy to do was to run out of the
   house.
   should
   It seemed to me that .... run out of the house.

Before you read

1 Reading pictures

Look at the picture on pages 30-31. Look closely at the buildings in the background on the left and at the billboard in the foreground on the right. (A billboard is a large board where people put posters to advertise things.) Then, in pairs or small groups, talk about the following:

- Describe the landscape. Think of one or two adjectives to describe your general impression: how does the landscape make you feel?
- Think about the people who live and work in the coffee shop and the garage. What do you think these people are like?
- What does the poster on the billboard advertise?
- What effect does the advertiser want to have on the public, do you think?
- Could the poster have a different effect from what the advertiser wanted? What effect does it have on you?

FCE 2 Fill in the gaps

Read the text below and think of the word which best fills each space. Use only <u>one</u> word in each space. There is an example at the beginning (0). Then read the first part of Chapter Two to check your answers.

About half way (0) ....between........ West Egg and New York the road joins the railroad and runs (1) .... it for a short distance to avoid a desolate area of land. This is a valley of ashes, (2) .... the gray land is always covered (3) .... clouds of dust.

Above the dust you (4) .... see the gigantic blue eyes of Doctor T. J. Eckleburg painted on a big board near the road. The eyes do not look out of a face (5) ...., instead, from a pair of enormous yellow glasses. Dr Eckleburg had probably moved (6) .... but the advertisement remained.

The train (7) .... here and that is (8) .... I met Tom Buchanan's mistress. Though I was interested (9) .... seeing her, I had no desire to meet her—but I did.

START

About half way between West Egg and New York the road joins the railroad and runs beside it for a short distance to avoid a desolate area of land. This is a valley of ashes, [1] where the gray land is always covered with clouds of dust.

Above the dust you can see the gigantic blue eyes of Doctor T. J. Eckleburg painted on a big board near the road. The eyes do not look out of a face but, instead, from a pair of enormous yellow glasses. Dr Eckleburg had probably moved away but the advertisement remained.

The train stops here and that is how I met Tom Buchanan's mistress. [2] Though I was interested in seeing her, I had no desire to meet her—but I did.

END

One Sunday afternoon I went to New York with Tom on the train and we stopped by the ash piles. [3] Tom jumped to his feet and said, "We're getting off. I want you to meet my girl." He took my arm and pulled me off the train.

I followed him to the only building in sight in this squalid land. There were three shops in the building. One was empty and another was a coffee shop. The third was a garage—REPAIRS George B. Wilson-cars bought and sold.

I followed Tom to the empty, dirty garage. The owner was a pale,

1. **ashes** : soft, gray powder that remains after burning something.
2. **mistress** : a woman in a sexual relationship with a man who is not her husband.
3. **piles** : (here) small hills.

miserable-looking man.

"Hello, Wilson," said Tom. "How's business?"

"Not bad," said Wilson sadly. "When are you going to sell me that car?"

"Next week. I've got my man working on it."

Tom looked around impatiently and in a moment the rather heavy figure of a woman appeared. She was in her mid-thirties and certainly not beautiful, but she was very sensual. [1]

She smiled slowly and, ignoring her husband, shook hands with Tom, looking at him straight in the eye.

"Get some chairs so we can sit down," she said to her husband, who hurried to get them.

"I want to see you," said Tom. "Get on the next train."

"All right."

"I'll meet you at the newspaper shop."

We waited for her down the road.

"Terrible place, isn't it?" said Tom. "It's good for her to get away. I rent an apartment in New York for her where we meet."

"Doesn't her husband say anything?"

"Wilson? He thinks she goes to see her sister in New York. He's so stupid he'll believe anything."

So Tom Buchanan, his girl and I rode the train to New York. Outside the station we got into a taxi and drove off. But she immediately stopped the taxi.

"I want one of those dogs. I want to get one for the apartment. It's nice to have a dog."

We stopped near a man with a basket full of young dogs.

"What kind are they?" asked Mrs Wilson.

---

1. **sensual** : she seemed to like physical pleasure.

"All kinds. What kind do you want?"

"I'd like a police dog. I don't suppose you have any."

The man looked doubtfully in the basket and pulled up one of the dogs.

"That's not a police dog," said Tom.

"No, it's not exactly a police dog," said the man.

"I think it's cute,"[1] said Mrs Wilson enthusiastically. "How much is it?"

"Ten dollars," the man said.

"Is it a boy or a girl?" she asked.

"That dog's a boy."

"It's a girl," said Tom firmly. "Here's your money. Go and buy ten more dogs with it."

We drove over to Fifth Avenue and I said, "I have to leave you here."

"No, you don't," Tom said quickly. "Myrtle wants you to come up to the apartment, don't you Myrtle?"

"Come on, I'll telephone my sister Catherine, who's quite beautiful. And I'm going to invite the McKees from the apartment below."

The apartment was on 158th Street, on the top floor. The small living room was crowded with large, decorated furniture.

Mrs Wilson sent a boy out to get milk, dog food and a box for the dog, while Tom opened a cupboard and brought out a bottle of whiskey.

I have been drunk only twice in my life and the second time was that afternoon, so everything that happened is still a bit hazy[2] to me. Mrs Wilson was sitting on Tom's knees as she telephoned several people. There were no cigarettes and I went out to buy some at the

---

1. **cute** : pleasing to look at.

2. **hazy** : unclear, vague.

drugstore. [1] When I came back they had both disappeared so I sat down in the living room and waited. Just as Tom and Myrtle came out of the bedroom, the guests began to arrive.

The sister, Catherine, was an attractive girl of about thirty. Mr McKee was a pale man from the apartment below. His wife had a loud, unpleasant voice.

Catherine sat down next to me on the couch.

"Do you live on Long Island, too?" she asked.

"I live at West Egg."

"Really? I was there at a party about a month ago. It was given by a man named Gatsby. Do you know him?"

"I live next door to him."

"Well, they say he's a relative of King Wilhelm of Germany. That's where all his money comes from."

"Really?"

Catherine looked at Tom and Myrtle and then whispered to me, "Myrtle and Tom both hate the people they're married to. They should get a divorce and marry each other! It's really his wife that's keeping them apart. She's a Catholic and they don't believe in divorce."

Daisy was not a Catholic and I was a little shocked at Tom's lie.

"She really should get away from her husband. They've been living over that garage for eleven years. And Tom's the first sweetheart [2] she's had."

The second bottle of whiskey was in constant demand by everybody except Catherine, who "felt just as good on nothing at all". We all had sandwiches, which were a complete supper. I wanted to

---

1. **drugstore** : in the USA, a pharmacy that sells not only medicines, but also health and beauty products, food, drinks and newspapers.
2. **sweetheart** : someone you love.

get out and walk toward the park, but each time I tried to go I became involved in some loud argument. [1]

Myrtle pulled her chair close to mine and suddenly her warm breath told me the story of her first meeting with Tom.

"I was on the train going to New York to see my sister and Tom was sitting on the seat in front of me. He was wearing an elegant suit and black leather shoes and I couldn't keep my eyes off him. But every time he looked at me, I looked at the advertisement over his head. When we came into the station he was next to me and his body was pressing against me. So I told him I'd have to call a policeman, but he knew I didn't mean it. I was so excited when I got into a taxi with him that I kept thinking, 'You can't live forever, you can't live forever.'"

She turned to Mrs McKee and she laughed her artificial laugh.

It was nine o'clock and almost immediately afterwards I looked at my watch and it was ten o'clock. The little dog was sitting on the table looking blindly through the smoke.

Tom and Mrs Wilson stood face to face discussing whether Mrs Wilson could mention Daisy's name.

"Daisy, Daisy, Daisy!" she shouted. "I'll say it whenever I want to! Daisy! Dai—"

Making a short, agile movement Tom Buchanan broke her nose with his open hand. There were bloody towels on the bathroom floor, women's voices everywhere and, above all the confusion, a long, broken cry of pain. Mr McKee and I went out the door.

"Come to lunch some day," he suggested as we went down in the elevator.

"All right," I agreed. "I'll be glad to."

---

1. **argument** : disagreement, a difference of opinion.

The text and **beyond**

FCE **1** **Characters**

Answer the questions by choosing from the characters (A-E). There is an example at the beginning (0).

A Nick   **B** Tom   **C** George Wilson   **D** Myrtle Wilson   **E** Catherine

0 Who did not really want to meet Myrtle? ....A........

1 Who wants to buy Tom's car? ....

2 Who rents an apartment in New York City? ....

3 Who wants to have a dog? ....

4 Who got drunk for the second time in his/her life that afternoon? ....

5 Who thinks Gatsby is related to King Wilhelm of Germany? ....

6 Who lied about Daisy's religion? ....

7 Who was shocked by the lie? ....

8 Who met Myrtle on a train? ....

9 Who broke Myrtle's nose? ....

'I don't suppose you have any.'

Look at these direct questions.

— *Do you have any police dogs?*
— *When does the train leave?*
— *Where is the post office?*
— *Did he leave early?*
— *Does the bus for Brooklyn stop here?*

To ask for information politely we use indirect questions.

— *I wonder (or I was wondering) if you have any police dogs.*
— *Do you have any idea when the train leaves?*
— *I don't suppose you know where the post office is.*
— *Do you know whether (or if) he left early?*
— *Could you please tell me whether (or if) the bus for Brooklyn stops here?*

Notice that when direct questions change to indirect questions, the word order changes and the auxiliary verb disappears:

Do you have any police dogs? ⇒ *... you have any police dogs.*
When does the train leave? ⇒ *... when the train leaves.*

If the direct question is a yes/no question and has no question word then we use "whether" or "if" in the indirect question.

Did he leave early? ⇒ *... whether he left early.*

❷ Polite questions

Change the following direct questions into more polite, indirect questions using the expression given.

1 Are there any more newspapers? ⇒
   I wonder ....
2 Where is the airport? ⇒
   Do you know ....
3 Do you have any fresh eggs? ⇒
   I wonder ....
4 Is the train to East Egg on time? ⇒
   I don't suppose you know ....
5 Does Jay still live in that mansion? ⇒
   Do you have any idea ....
6 When does the restaurant open? ⇒
   Could you please tell me ....
7 Does that store sell newspapers? ⇒
   Do you know ....
8 Why hasn't she come yet? ⇒
   I don't suppose you know ....

❸ Discussion

1 Why do you think that Nick is not surprised that Tom had a mistress but is surprised that he got upset over a book?
2 Why do you think Nick is shocked that Tom told Myrtle that Daisy was a Catholic?
3 What do you think Tom's lying about Daisy says about Tom?

4 You can't live forever

Explain why Myrtle kept saying to herself "You can't live forever. You can't live forever."

Before you read

FCE **1** Gatsby's parties

Read the first part of Chapter Three. For questions 1-6, choose the best answer — A, B, C or D.

1 How did Gatsby bring people from the city to his party?

A ☐ by bus
B ☐ in his Rolls-Royce
C ☐ by train
D ☐ in his motorboat

2 How often did Gatsby have a party?

A ☐ at least once a week
B ☐ at least once every two weeks
C ☐ at least once every three weeks
D ☐ once a month

3 How was Nick different from most of the other guests at the party?

A ☐ He had received an invitation.
B ☐ He had come uninvited.
C ☐ He had come with somebody else's invitation.
D ☐ He had been driven by Gatsby's chauffeur.

4 What did Nick wear to the party?

A ☐ a dark blue jacket and white trousers
B ☐ a light blue uniform
C ☐ a light blue suit
D ☐ a white jacket and blue trouser

5 What did Nick think that the well-dressed young Englishmen were trying to do?

A ☐ sell something
B ☐ meet Gatsby
C ☐ talk to Jordan Baker
D ☐ eat something

6 What did Gatsby do when the girl tore her dress?

A ☐ He repaired the dress and gave it to her.
B ☐ He gave her $265.
C ☐ He went to visit her.
D ☐ He gave her a new dress.

START

There was music from my neighbor's house through the summer nights. In his gardens men and girls came and went, drifting among the champagne and the stars. In the afternoon I watched his guests swimming or taking the sun on the hot beach, while his motorboats raced across the water.

On weekends his Rolls-Royce became a bus, carrying people to and from the city, between nine in the morning and long past midnight. He went to meet all the trains at the station.

On Mondays eight servants worked all day to repair the damage of the night before.

At least once every two weeks preparations were made for a huge party. There were colored lights, a dance floor on the lawn and an orchestra that played dance music. The buffet tables were covered with all kinds of fine food. A bar was set up with every possible kind of alcoholic drink. And everywhere there were waiters ready to serve the guests. There was a general sense of excitement in the air. As the sky grew darker, the lights grew brighter. Minute by minute the laughter increased. The guests moved about talking, smiling, dancing, eating, drinking and laughing.

I believe that on the first night I went to Gatsby's house I was one of the few guests who had received an invitation. People were not invited—they just went to his parties. They got into automobiles that took them to Long Island and somehow they arrived at Gatsby's door. Sometimes they were

introduced to Gatsby and sometimes they came and went and never met Gatsby.

I had actually been invited. A driver in a light blue uniform crossed my lawn early that Saturday morning with a surprisingly formal invitation signed by Jay Gatsby.

Dressed in white trousers and a dark blue jacket, I went over to his lawn a little after seven. I wandered around, ill-at-ease,[1] among all those people I didn't know. I was surprised by the number of well-dressed young Englishmen who looked a little hungry and talked in low voices to solid, prosperous Americans. I was sure they were all trying to sell something, since they were aware of the easy money that surrounded them.

As soon as I arrived I tried to find my host by asking some of the guests but they stared[2] at me in amazement. So I went to the cocktail table—the only place where a single man could stay without looking out of place.

After a while Jordan Baker came out of the house and stood at the top of the marble steps looking at the garden.

"Hello!" I shouted, looking towards her.

"I thought you might be here," she answered absently. "I remembered that you lived next door to—"

Two girls in yellow dresses interrupted her.

"Hello!" they cried together. "Sorry you didn't win."

That was for the golf tournament. She had lost in the finals the week before. With Jordan's slender golden arm resting on mine, we went down the marble steps and walked around the

---

1. **ill-at-ease** : feeling uncomfortable.
2. **stared** : looked with wide-open eyes.

garden. We sat down at a table with the two girls in yellow and three men.

"I like to come to these parties," said one girl. "I don't care what I do, so I always have a good time. When I was here last time I tore my dress on a chair, and he asked me my name and address. After a week I received a package with a new evening dress in it. Two hundred and sixty-five dollars!"

"There's something strange about a man who will do a thing like that," said the other girl. "He doesn't want any trouble with anybody."

"Who doesn't?" I asked.

"Gatsby. Someone told me he killed a man once," said one of the girls.

An air of excitement came over us.

"I heard that he was a German spy during the war," said one of the men.

"Oh, no," said a girl, "he was in the American army during the war."

We all turned and looked around for Gatsby, the man everyone whispered about.

Supper was being served and Jordan invited me to join her group of friends on the other side of the garden. They were a respectable group of people from East Egg who did not want to mix with the other guests.

"Let's get out," whispered Jordan after half an hour. "This is much too polite for me."

We got up and Jordan explained that we wanted to find the host, since I had never met him.

The bar where we looked first was crowded but Gatsby was not there. We tried in several places but could not find him.

43

Then we tried an important-looking door and walked into a great Gothic library.

A fat, middle-aged man with enormous round glasses was sitting on a great table. He was rather drunk and was staring at the books.

When we entered he looked at us excitedly.

"What do you think?" he asked.

"About what?"

He waved his hand toward the bookshelves.

"About the books. They're real! I thought they weren't, but they're real! They have pages and everything." He pulled down a heavy book and opened it.

"I've been drunk for about a week now, and I thought I might feel better if I sat in the library."

We went back outside. There was dancing in the garden now. Happy explosions of laughter rose toward the summer sky and became louder as the night went on.

I was still with Jordan Baker. We were sitting at a table with a man of about my age and a loud girl. I was enjoying myself now. I drank two glasses of champagne and the scene became deep and significant.

The man looked at me and smiled.

"Your face is familiar," he said politely. "Weren't you in the Third Division during the war?"

"Why, yes!"

We talked for a while about some wet, gray little villages in France. He evidently lived nearby because he told me that he had just bought a hydroplane and was going to try it out in the morning.

"Want to go with me, old sport?" [1]

"What time?"

"Any time that's best for you."

I wanted to ask his name when Jordan looked around and smiled.

"Having a good time now?"

"Much better."

I turned again to my new friend. "This is an unusual party for me. I haven't seen the host. I live over there—" and I waved my hand toward my house, "and this man Gatsby sent over his driver with an invitation."

"I'm Gatsby," he said suddenly.

"What!" I exclaimed. "Oh, I'm so sorry!"

"I thought you knew, old sport. I'm afraid I'm not a very good host."

He smiled understandingly. It was one of those rare smiles with a quality of reassurance [2] in it that you see four or five times in your life. Then the smile vanished and I was looking at an elegant young man, a year or two over thirty, whose formal way of speaking was almost absurd.

At this moment a butler informed him that Chicago was calling him on the telephone.

"Excuse me. I will join you later."

When he was gone I turned immediately to Jordan to tell her of my surprise. I had expected Gatsby to be a robust, older man.

---

1. **old sport** : 'boy', 'man', 'friend'. When Gatsby uses this expression he wants to be friendly. He is the only person in the story who uses this expression, so it becomes associated with him.
2. **reassurance** : encouragement, comfort.

"Who is he?" I demanded.

"He's just a man named Gatsby."

"Where is he from? What does he do?"

"Now *you're* on the subject," she said with a weak smile. "Well, he told me once that he had been to Oxford University, but I don't believe it."

"Why not?"

"I don't know. I just don't think he went there."

If someone had told me that Gatsby came from the swamps [1] of Louisiana or the lower East Side of New York I would have believed it. But I couldn't believe that a young man can come from nowhere and buy a palace on Long Island.

As the orchestra played, I looked at Gatsby, who was standing alone on the steps looking at one group and then another with approving eyes. His tanned [2] skin was smooth and his short hair looked like it was cut every day. I could see nothing mysterious about him.

Suddenly Gatsby's butler was standing beside us.

"Miss Baker?" he asked. "I beg your pardon, but Mr Gatsby would like to speak to you alone."

"With me?" she exclaimed in surprise.

"Yes, madam."

She got up slowly and followed the butler.

I was alone and it was almost two o'clock. As time went on the party became noisier. I decided it was time to go home.

As I waited for my hat in the hall, the door of the library

---

1. **swamps** : soft, wet lands with much vegetation, insects and reptiles.
2. **tanned** : brownish color given to the skin by the sunlight.

opened and Jordan Baker and Gatsby came out together. He was talking to her enthusiastically.

"I've just heard the most surprising thing," she whispered. "How long were we in there?"

"About an hour."

"It was simply amazing," she repeated. "But I promised I wouldn't tell it. Come and see me... phone book... under the name of Mrs Sigourney Howard... my aunt... " She hurried away as she talked.

I was rather ashamed that on my first visit I had stayed so late. I tried to explain to Gatsby that I had looked for him all evening.

"Don't mention it," he said eagerly. "And don't forget we're going up in the hydroplane tomorrow morning at nine o'clock."

Then the butler said, "Philadelphia wants you on the phone."

"All right, I'll be there in a minute. Good night, old sport."

Reading over what I have written so far, I see that I have given the impression that the events of those three nights were all that interested me. On the contrary, they were only some of the events in a crowded summer. They became important only much later.

I worked in New York at the Probity Trust most of the time and I began to like the city. For a while I didn't see Jordan Baker and then in midsummer I found her again. At first I liked to go out with her because she was a golf champion and everyone knew her name. Then it was something more. I wasn't in love but I felt a sort of desire to get to know her better.

The bored, arrogant face that she showed the world hid

something, and one day I discovered what it was. When we were at a party at Warwick she left a borrowed car out in the rain with the top down, and then she lied about it. Suddenly I remembered a story about her. At her first big golf tournament there had been a scandal that almost reached the newspapers—a suggestion that she had moved her ball to a better position in order to win.

She was incurably dishonest. She used dishonesty to get what she wanted and continued to smile proudly to the world.

It made no difference to me. Dishonesty in a woman is something you learn to accept—I was sorry and then I forgot about it.

It was at the same party that I had a curious conversation about driving a car. It started because she passed too close to some workmen and almost touched one.

"You're a bad driver. You should either be careful or you should not drive at all," I said.

"I am careful."

"No, you're not."

"Well, other people are," she said.

"Suppose you meet someone as careless as you?"

"I hope I never will. I hate careless people. That's why I like you."

Her gray eyes stared straight ahead, but she had made a change in our relationship, and for a moment I thought I loved her. But I am full of rules that stop me from doing what I want. I knew that I had to break off the relationship with the girl back home before I was free. I am one of the few honest people I have ever known.

The text and **beyond**

1 Comprehension check

Say whether the following sentences are True (T), False (F) or Possibly True (P).

		T	F	P
1	Gatsby went to meet his guests at the train station.	☐	☐	☐
2	Gatsby knew all the people who came to his parties.	☐	☐	☐
3	Gatsby sent a girl a new dress because she had torn hers at one of his parties.	☐	☐	☐
4	Gatsby was a German spy during the war.	☐	☐	☐
5	The fat man in the library was surprised that Gatsby had so many books.	☐	☐	☐
6	The man who asked Nick if he was in the Third Division was actually Gatsby.	☐	☐	☐
7	Nick had not expected Gatsby to be an elegant young man.	☐	☐	☐
8	Gatsby had been to Oxford University.	☐	☐	☐
9	In the beginning Nick liked going out with Jordan because she was famous.	☐	☐	☐
10	During her first major golf tournament Jordan had moved a ball in order to win.	☐	☐	☐
11	Nick was upset that Jordan lied.	☐	☐	☐
12	Nick considers himself an honest person.	☐	☐	☐

2 Discussion

1 Why do you think that the man with the round glasses was so surprised that the books in Gatsby's library were real?

2 What does Nick find to be absurd about Gatsby?

3 What strikes Nick the most about Gatsby?

4 How is Nick different from Jordan?

'In his gardens men and girls came and went, drifting among the champagne and the stars.'

One common use of -ing clauses is to describe a longer action that is happening at the same time as the main verb.

Look at these two sentences below with -ing clauses.

— *Men and girls came and went, drifting among the champagne and the stars.* ⇒ *Men and girls came and went, and, at the same time, they drifted among the champagne and the stars.*

— *The guests moved about, talking, smiling, dancing, eating, drinking and laughing.* ⇒ *The guests moved about, and, at the same time, they talked, smiled, danced, ate, drank and laughed.*

3 Combining sentences

Combine the two sentences to form one sentence with an -ing clause. One of the verbs in brackets must be in the Past Simple and the other must become an -ing clause.

Example: She (cook) dinner. She (burn) herself.
          She burnt herself cooking dinner.

1   Gatsby (fight) in the war. Gatsby (receive) many medals.
    ....

2   Nick (walk) around the grounds of Gatsby's mansion. Nick (be) ill-at-ease.
    ....

3   "Good morning," she (say). She (look) towards me.
    ....

4   Nick (sit) at a table with a man and a loud girl. Nick (enjoy) himself.
    ....

5   Gatsby (smoke) his pipe. Gatsby (look) out towards the green light.
    ....

6   She (listen) to the music. She (tap) her feet.
    ....

7   I (get) lost. I (go) home.
    ....

51

'He was rather drunk and was staring at the books.'

4 Vocabulary – verbs of seeing

A   Here are four definitions of verbs that describe different ways of seeing and looking. Say which of these definitions best describes the verbs in italics in the sentences below.

A   to look at for a long time because of curiosity or surprise
B   to observe
C   to look at quickly and secretly, often through a small opening
D   to see for a moment

1   The little boy *peeped* at the man from behind the curtains.
2   I *watched* the boys as they were playing football.
3   He *glimpsed* the driver as the car raced past on the road.
4   I *stared* at the movie star with amazement because I had never seen a movie star before.

B   Now fill in the gaps with the appropriate verb. Each verb may be used more than once.

1   I .... through the keyhole and saw John who was talking on the phone.
2   She was .... a film on television when the phone rang.
3   I .... a strange man walking among those trees, but he was gone before I could see his face.
4   Why are you .... at me? Is there something on my face?
5   The shy little girl .... at the little boy from behind the statue.
6   I could not stop .... at her because she was so incredibly beautiful.

5 Discussion

What do you think of Gatsby?

The "Roaring Twenties"

The 1920s were a period of social change and tension in the United States. After World War One the United States wanted to return to pre-war normality, which meant isolationism. [1] America did not want to become involved in problems with other countries.

While many Americans remained tied to the old values of family, home, church and hard work, a new cosmopolitan, urban America was growing up in big cities among the young upper-middle class and the rich. The social and cultural conflict was very strong.

A new hedonistic [2] way of life was becoming fashionable, particularly on college campuses [3] on the East Coast. Fitzgerald's novel *This Side of Paradise* (1920) told of wild parties, heavy drinking and

1. **isolationism** : a policy of not having close relations with other countries.
2. **hedonistic** : thinking that pleasure is the most important thing in life.
3. **campuses** : the land surrounding a university or college.

sexual freedom among the young people at Princeton University. By contrast, Sinclair Lewis's critical novel *Main Street* (1920) was a caricature of the boring, prudish, [1] banal small-town life of the American Midwest, tied to old values.

Perhaps the most evident changes of the twenties regarded young women. In 1919 women's skirts were about six inches above the ground. In the 1920s they were at the knees! The new modern woman had short hair, wore colorful, innovative clothes, used cosmetics, smoked cigarettes, danced to the rhythm of jazz bands, went to wild parties and drank alcoholic drinks. This was an open rebellion against the values of the past, and most parents and older people were shocked. Moreover, thanks to canned food, [2] ready-made clothing and household appliances, [3] middle and upper-middle-class women were freed from a lot of household work and began working away from home.

This was a period of general prosperity and social change. Henry Ford put Americans on wheels

1. **prudish** : narrow-minded, particularly about sexual matters.
2. **canned food** : (American expression) food in tins.
3. **household appliances** : small machines, often electrical, which do housework.

with his revolutionary Model T Ford, the car everyone could afford to buy. People were spending more money on travel, vacations and having fun.

Newspapers, magazines and a fast-growing radio industry changed the nature of communications and information. This was the beginning of "sensationalism" [1] in the mass media, which was a revolution in itself.

In 1919 a new law prohibited the sale of alcoholic beverages in America. Many Americans did not agree with this limitation of personal freedom. They ignored the new law and drank alcohol in secret, illegal clubs called "speakeasies". The term "speakeasy" was used for the first time in a newspaper article about an old Irish woman who sold liquor illegally. In the early 1900s the word "easy" meant softly. The term she used with her clients was "speak easy", so that the police would not find out!

Bootlegging [2] became an extremely profitable, illegal business. Bootleggers and gangsters became very rich in a short time. Crime increased suddenly and gang wars and shootings became common.

1. **"sensationalism"** : the intentional creation of excitement and shock in newspapers and magazines.
2. **bootlegging** : making and selling illegal goods; in this case, alcoholic drinks.

Al Capone from Chicago, the most notorious gangster of the 1920s, made millions of dollars from bootlegging and other illegal activities. In 1933 the law was abolished.

The carefree [1] life of the "Roaring Twenties" ended suddenly on October 29, 1929, when the New York Stock Exchange fell dramatically. Banks, businesses and people became bankrupt overnight. America was entering the dark period of the Great Depression, which had a profound effect not only on the United States but all over the world.

1 Comprehension check

Answer the following questions.

1 What did "isolationism" mean?
2 What kind of lifestyle was described in Fitzgerald's novel *This Side of Paradise*?
3 What kind of lifestyle was described in Lewis's novel *Main Street*?
4 How did the lives of many women change during this period?
5 How did Henry Ford change the lives of ordinary Americans?
6 What were "speakeasies"?
7 Why were they set up?
8 What happened on October 29, 1929?

2 Discussion

- What were the 1920s like in *your* country?
- What other decade(s) was/were significant in your country in the 20th century?
- Do you give a special name to this/these decade(s)? For example, for Americans the 1920s are the "Roaring Twenties", and for the British the 1960s are the "Swinging Sixties".

1. **carefree** : without problems or worries, happy.

Before you read

1 Gatsby's background

A   Several people in the story — including Nick — don't believe what Gatsby tells them about his background. Why do you think this is — why might people not believe Gatsby?

B   When you have done activity 2 below, stop for a moment before you continue reading. Do any of the eight statements seem difficult to believe? If so, why? And if so, how does this affect your view of Gatsby?

2 Read the first part of Chapter Four and complete the following sentences with the missing information. You will need a word or a short phrase.

1   This was the first time that Gatsby had ever ....
....

2   After talking to Gatsby several times Nick was disappointed because he discovered that Gatsby had ....
....

3   Gatsby said that his family was from the Midwest and that now they were all ....
....

4   Gatsby went to Oxford because it was a ....
....

5   When Gatsby's family died he received ....
....

6   Gatsby told Nick about his life in Europe but Nick did not
....

7   Gatsby said that during the war he had tried very hard to
....

8   Gatsby said that during the war every major government gave him
....

START

At nine o'clock one morning in July, Gatsby's splendid car stopped outside my door. It was the first time he had visited me, although I had gone to two of his parties, flown on his hydroplane and used his beach many times.

"Good morning, old sport. You're having lunch with me today and I thought we'd drive to town together."

He saw me looking with admiration at his car.

"It's pretty, isn't it? Haven't you seen it before?"

I'd seen it before. Everybody had seen it. It was huge and shiny: a rich, cream color with green leather seats.

I had talked to him several times in the past month and found, to my disappointment, that he had little to say. At first I thought he was an interesting person, but now he was simply the owner of the elaborate house next door.

And then came that perplexing [1] ride. Gatsby seemed strangely ill-at-ease.

"Listen, old sport," he said suddenly, "what's your opinion of me?"

I was a bit surprised and I started making some very general comments.

"Well," he interrupted, "I'm going to tell you something about my life. I don't want you to get the wrong idea of me

---

1. **perplexing** : difficult to understand.

58

from all these stories you hear."

So he was aware of the stories that were told about him.

"I'll tell you God's truth. I am the son of some wealthy people in the Midwest—all dead now. I was brought up in America, but educated at Oxford because it's a family tradition."

He looked at me sideways and I knew why Jordan Baker had thought he was lying. He hurried the phrase "educated at Oxford", as if it bothered [1] him.

"What part of the Midwest?"

"San Francisco."

"I see."

"My family all died and I received a good amount of money. After that I lived like a prince in all the capitals of Europe—in Paris, Venice, Rome—collecting jewels, hunting wild animals, painting a little and trying to forget something very sad that had happened to me long ago."

I tried not to laugh. I couldn't believe a word of what he was saying.

"Then came the war, old sport. I was so glad and I tried very hard to die but I didn't. I became an officer when the war began. After some time and several battles, I was promoted to major and every government gave me a medal—even little Montenegro on the Adriatic Sea."

He smiled, reached in his pocket and pulled out a piece of metal on a ribbon.

"That's the one from Montenegro."

To my great surprise the thing looked authentic: "Major Jay Gatsby—For Extraordinary Courage."

---

1. **bothered** : annoyed, troubled.

"Here's another thing I always carry. A souvenir of Oxford days. It was taken at Trinity College."

It was a photo of six young men, with old buildings in the background. There was Gatsby looking a little, not much, younger.

Then it was all true.

"I'm going to make a big request of you today," he said, "so I thought you should know something about me. I don't want you to think that I'm a nobody. You see I usually drift here and there among strangers trying to forget the sad thing that happened to me. But you'll hear about it this afternoon."

"At lunch?"

"No, this afternoon. I found out that you're taking Miss Baker to tea."

"Do you mean you are in love with Miss Baker?"

"No, old sport, I'm not. But Miss Baker has agreed to talk to you about this matter." [1]

I had no idea what "this matter" was but I was more annoyed than interested. I had not asked Jordan to tea to talk about Mr Jay Gatsby.

He wouldn't say a word. We drove on and we approached the valley of the ashes. I saw Mrs Wilson working at the gas [2] pump with her usual vitality.

I met Gatsby for lunch in a little restaurant on Forty-Second Street. He was talking to a small man with a flat nose, a large head and small eyes.

---

1. **matter** : (here) subject.

2. **gas** : (U.S.) gasoline, petrol.

"Mr Carraway, this is my friend Mr Wolfshiem."

"This is a nice restaurant," said Mr Wolfshiem, "but I like the old Metropole better."

"It's too hot over there," said Gatsby.

"Hot and small—yes," said Mr Wolfshiem, "but full of memories; it's filled with faces dead and gone. I'll never forget that Rosy Rosenthal was shot there. There were six of us at the table. When it was almost morning, the waiter went to him with a strange look and said that someone wanted to speak to him outside. I told him not to go."

"Did he go?" I asked innocently.

"Sure, he went out into the street and they shot him three times in his full stomach and drove away."

He looked at me and said, "I understand you're looking for a business connection."

Gatsby answered for me.

"Oh, no. This isn't the man! We'll talk about that another time."

Towards the end of the meal Gatsby looked at his watch and hurried out of the room.

"He has to telephone," said Mr Wolfshiem. "Fine man, isn't he? He's handsome and is a perfect gentleman. He's an Oggsford[1] man."

"Have you known Gatsby for a long time?" I asked.

"Several years. I met him after the war and I knew he was a fine man."

When Gatsby came back, Mr Wolfshiem left and Gatsby

---

1. **Oggsford** : the way Mr. Wolfshiem pronounces 'Oxford' shows that he has a lower-class background.

said, "He's quite a character [1] around New York."

"Who is he—an actor?"

"Meyer Wolfshiem? No, he's a gambler. [2] He was responsible for the big sports scandal of 1919."

"And why isn't he in prison?"

"They can't get him. He's too smart." [3]

I insisted on paying for the lunch and then I saw Tom Buchanan across the crowded room.

"Come with me for a minute," I said to Gatsby. "I've got to say hello to someone."

When he saw us Tom jumped up. "Where've you been? Daisy's angry because you haven't telephoned."

"This is Mr Gatsby, Mr Buchanan."

They shook hands and a look of embarrassment came over Gatsby's face.

"How have you been?" asked Tom. "How did you happen to come here to eat?"

"I've been having lunch with Mr Gatsby—"

I turned toward Mr Gatsby, but he was no longer there.

That afternoon, in the tea garden at the Plaza Hotel, Jordan Baker told me this story, which took place in Louisville, a small Midwest town where she grew up.

One October day in 1917 (said Jordan Baker) I was walking along the street where Daisy Fay lived. She was eighteen, two years older than me, and was the most popular young girl in

---

1. **character** : (here) an eccentric or strange individual.
2. **gambler** : a person who plays cards or other games for money.
3. **smart** : (here) clever, intelligent.

Louisville. She dressed in white and had a little white car. All day long the telephone rang in her house and excited young officers wanted to take her out that night.

That morning when I was near her house she was sitting in her white car with an officer I had never seen before. They were so interested in each other that she didn't see me until I was near them.

"Hello, Jordan," she called. "Please come here."

She asked me if I was going to the Red Cross that afternoon. I was. Well, then, could I tell them that she couldn't come that day? The officer looked at Daisy while I was speaking in a way that every girl wants to be looked at some time. His name was Jay Gatsby and I didn't see him again for over four years. Even after I had met him on Long Island, I didn't realize it was the same man.

That was 1917. By the next year I had a few young men too,

and I began to play in tournaments so I didn't see Daisy very often. She went with a slightly older group.

By the next autumn she was happy again and in June she married Tom Buchanan of Chicago with a ceremony that Louisville had never seen before and rented the entire floor of the hotel. The day before the wedding he gave her a string of pearls [1] worth $350,000.

I was a bridesmaid [2] at her wedding. I went into her room half an hour before the big dinner and found her lying on the bed as lovely as the June night and very drunk. She had a bottle in her hand and a letter in the other.

"Never had a drink before," she said.

"What's the matter, Daisy?"

I was scared because I had never seen a girl like that before.

"Here." She put her hand in a wastebasket and pulled out a string of pearls. "Take them downstairs and give them back to who they belong to. Tell them 'Daisy's changed her mind!'"

She began to cry—she cried and cried. I found her mother's maid and we locked the door and put her into a cold bath. She kept the letter with her until it became a wet ball.

But she didn't say another word and half an hour later she walked out of the room with the pearls around her neck. The next day at five o'clock she married Tom Buchanan and left for a three-month trip to the South Seas.

I saw them in Santa Barbara when they returned and thought I'd never seen a girl so crazy about her husband. If he

---

1. **string of pearls** :

2. **bridesmaid** : the bride's female attendant.

left the room for a minute she'd look around uneasily and say, "Where's Tom gone?" She used to sit on the sand with his head on her knee, looking at him with immense delight. That was August. A week after I left Santa Barbara, Tom had a car accident. There was a girl with him who broke her arm. This was Tom's first affair.

The next April Daisy had a child and they went to live in France for a year. Then they returned to Chicago to settle down. [1] They moved with a fast [2] group—all of them young, rich and wild. But Daisy's reputation remained perfect. Perhaps because she doesn't drink.

Well, about six weeks ago she heard the name Gatsby for the first time in years. It was when I asked you if you knew Gatsby in West Egg. After you had gone home she came into my room and woke me up and said, "What Gatsby?" And when I described him she said in a strange voice that it must be the man she used to know. It wasn't until then that I connected this Gatsby with the officer in her white car.

When Jordan Baker had finished telling all this, we had left the Plaza and we were driving through Central Park.

"It was a strange coincidence that brought him so near her," I said.

"But it wasn't a coincidence at all."

"Why not?"

---

1. **settle down** : decide to live in a place for a long time.
2. **fast** : (here) enjoying an active, expensive and often dangerous way of life.

"Gatsby bought that house so that Daisy would be just across the bay."

Then it had not been the stars which seemed to fill him with such feeling. Now he came alive to me.

"He wants to know if you'll invite Daisy to your house some afternoon and then let him come over."

I was amazed that he should ask so little. He had waited five years and bought a magnificent house so that he could "come over"[1] some afternoon to a stranger's garden.

"Why didn't he ask you to arrange a meeting?"

"He wants her to see his house. And your house is next door. I think he actually expected her to go to one of his parties, but she never did. Then he started asking people if they knew her. And I was the first one he found."

"Does Daisy want to see Gatsby?" I asked.

"She mustn't know. You have to just invite her to tea."

It was dark now and I put my arm around Jordan's golden shoulder and pulled her toward me and asked her to dinner.

---

1. **come over** : come to someone's house to visit.

The text and **beyond**

1 Comprehension check

Answer the following questions.

1   What was Gatsby's car like?
2   Why did Gatsby say that he wanted to tell Nick about his life?
3   Why did Gatsby try to die during the war?
4   How did Gatsby try to prove to Nick that he had actually been a war hero and studied at Oxford?
5   What happened to Rosy Rosenthal?
6   According to Gatsby, what did Mr Wolfshiem do for a living?
7   Why didn't Wolfshiem go to prison after the big sports scandal of 1919?
8   How did Gatsby react when he met Tom Buchanan?
9   Where did Jordan Baker see Jay Gatsby for the first time?
10 What was he doing when she saw him?
11 When Jordan saw Daisy just before the wedding, what did Daisy ask her to do?
12 What did Gatsby want Nick to do for him?

2 Discussion

1   Why do you think Daisy constantly said "Where's Tom gone?"?
2   Why did Gatsby throw all his magnificent parties?
3   What does Nick mean when he says about Gatsby, "Now he came alive to me."?

T: GRADE 7
3 Topic – village and city life

1   Where can you eat traditional dishes in your village or town?
2   Describe your favorite restaurant and its menu.
2   Some people say the most traditional dishes are eaten in the home. Do you agree? (Why/why not?)

FCE ④ The scandal of the 1919 World Series

Read the article on the 1919 World Series. For questions 1-4, choose the correct answers — A, B, C or D.

Baseball has always been America's "national pastime" and despite the millions of dollars paid to its top players, it will always be associated with a kind of pastoral innocence, a time when Americans lived mostly in the countryside, before the corruption of the big cities. Hollywood has examined this theme in baseball many times: *The Natural* (1984) starring Robert Redford and *Field of Dreams* (1989) starring Kevin Costner. *Field of Dreams* deals directly with the 1919 World Series.

F. Scott Fitzgerald chose to present the scandal of the 1919 World Series as a key element in his novel *The Great Gatsby*. When the novel came out in 1925, the reader would have understood perfectly Gatsby's proud statement that his friend Wolfshiem "fixed" the World Series but was too smart to be caught. The scandal of the 1919 World Series represented a kind of loss of national innocence.

The Chicago White Sox were going to play the Cincinnati Reds in the national baseball championship known as the World Series. The White Sox were the favorites to win, and most gamblers were going to bet on the White Sox victory. If the Reds could win, then the gamblers who knew about it would win enormous amounts of money.

Edward Victor Cicotte of the
Chicago White Sox.

This was the idea of the famous gambler and bookmaker, Joseph "Sport" Sullivan who, with one of the players of the White Sox, Arnold "Chick" Gandil, convinced the whole White Sox team to lose the World Series. This was not that difficult because these star players were paid very little money.

It was only after the White Sox lost

the World Series during the 1920 baseball season that rumors began to spread that the World Series had been fixed. The scandal became front-page news all across the nation and the White Sox became known as the "Black Sox".

One newspaper reported that when one of the star players, "Shoeless" Joe Jackson of the White Sox, was coming out of the courtroom, a little boy came up to him and said, "Say it ain't so, Joe!" (Joe, tell me that it isn't true!)

This phrase sums up the shock of a nation which had lost its innocence. In the end, all eight White Sox players involved in the scandal were banned from professional baseball forever or, we might say, forever chased from America's Garden of Eden.

1 How was the 1919 World Series scandal seen by many in the United States?

A ☐ as an example of the corruption of professional sports
B ☐ as an example of how the public can easily be fooled
C ☐ as the sad story of how money can buy anything
D ☐ as the loss of the nation's innocence

2 Why did gamblers want to fix the 1919 World Series?

A ☐ because Americans were so innocent nobody would discover the crime
B ☐ because if the White Sox lost, they could make a lot of money
C ☐ because players were not paid very much
D ☐ because baseball made more money than football or basketball

3 Why was it easy to convince the White Sox players to lose the World Series?

A ☐ The players needed money because their salaries were low.
B ☐ They didn't think they would be discovered.

C ☐ They did not care if they won or lost the World Series.

D ☐ Their best players were injured.

4 How was it discovered that the World Series had been fixed?

A ☐ after a court case

B ☐ from a newspaper reporter

C ☐ from the confessions of the gamblers

D ☐ because of the poor performance of the Chicago White Sox

Before you read

1 Meeting Daisy

Read the first part of Chapter Five and decide whether the following statements are true (T) or false (F).

		T	F
1	Gatsby's house was lit up because Gatsby was having another one of his huge parties.	☐	☐
2	Nick intended to invite Daisy to his house for tea the next day.	☐	☐
3	Gatsby wanted to have Nick's lawn cut.	☐	☐
4	Nick didn't earn a lot.	☐	☐
5	Nick accepted to work for Gatsby selling bonds.	☐	☐
6	Nick told Daisy not to bring Tom when she came for tea.	☐	☐
7	Gatsby arrived at Nick's house at three o'clock.	☐	☐
8	Daisy thought that Nick had invited her for tea because he was in love with her.	☐	☐
9	Gatsby hadn't seen Daisy for almost five years.	☐	☐

START 1

When I came home to West Egg at two o'clock that morning, I saw that Gatsby's entire house was brightly lit.

At first I thought it was another party, but there wasn't a sound, only the wind in the trees. Then I saw Gatsby walking toward me across the lawn.

"Your place looks like the World's Fair," [1] I said.

"Does it? I've been looking at some of the rooms." He waited and looked at me.

"I talked with Miss Baker," I said after a moment. "I'm going to phone Daisy tomorrow and invite her here to tea."

"Oh, that's all right," he said carelessly. "I don't want to put you to any trouble."

"What day is best for you?"

"What day is best for *you*?"

"How about the day after tomorrow at four o'clock."

He thought for a moment.

"I want to get the grass cut," he said.

We both looked at the grass—there was a line where my untidy lawn ended and his tidy one began. I suspected that he meant my grass.

2 "There's another little thing." He paused. "I thought—well, old sport, you don't make much money, do you?"

---

1. **World's Fair** : the most important international exhibition of that period.

"Not very much."

"I thought you didn't. Please pardon my—you see, I carry on a little business on the side. And I thought that if you don't make very much—you're selling bonds, aren't you?"

"Trying to."

"Well, this might interest you. It wouldn't take up much of your time and you could make some money; it's a rather confidential thing."

In a different situation that conversation could have changed my life. But I realized that he made the offer to repay me for the favor I was going to do him. I had to refuse.

"I've got my hands full,"[1] I said. "Thanks, but I couldn't take on any more work."

3 I phoned Daisy from the office the next morning and invited her to tea.

"Don't bring Tom," I told her.

"What?"

"Don't bring Tom."

On that day it was raining heavily. At eleven o'clock a man in a raincoat knocked at my door and said Mr Gatsby had sent him to cut the grass.

At two o'clock an enormous quantity of flowers arrived from Gatsby's. An hour later the front door opened and Gatsby, in a white suit, silver shirt and gold-colored tie, hurried in. He was pale and there were dark circles under his eyes.

"Is everything all right?" he asked.

"The grass looks fine, if that's what you mean."

---

1. **I've got my hands full** : I'm too busy to do anything else.

"What grass?" he asked. "Oh, the grass out there. Is everything ready for the tea?"

I took him to the kitchen. Together we examined the lemon cakes from the shop.

"They're fine," he said.

Gatsby sat down and looked vacantly [1] at one of my books. From time to time he looked at the window. Finally he got up and told me in an uncertain voice that he was going home.

"Why?"

"Nobody's coming to tea; it's too late!"

"Don't be silly. It's just two minutes to four."

4 He sat down unhappily and just then there was the sound of a car outside my house.

I went out and saw a big car. The driver stopped and Daisy's face, beneath a lavender [2] hat, looked at me with a joyful smile.

"Is this really where you live?"

Her voice was exhilarating.

"Are you in love with me?" she said softly in my ear. "Why did you ask me to come alone?"

"That's a secret. Tell your driver to go far away for an hour."

We went in. To my great surprise the living room was empty.

There was a light knocking at the front door. I went and opened it. Gatsby, pale as death, [3] with his hands in his coat

---

1. **vacantly** : showing lack of attention or interest.
2. **lavender** : a pale, purple color.
3. **pale as death** : his face was very white.

pockets, was standing there staring tragically into my eyes.

With his hands still in his coat pockets he marched in front of me and disappeared into the living room.

For half a minute there wasn't a sound. Then I heard a murmur and part of a laugh, followed by Daisy's voice.

"I'm certainly very glad to see you again," she said.

I had nothing to do in the hall so I went into the living room.

Gatsby, his hands still in his pockets, was leaning awkwardly [1] against the fireplace. Daisy was sitting gracefully but nervously on a chair.

"We've met before," said Gatsby in a low voice.

"We haven't met for many years," said Daisy in a flat voice.

"Five years next November," said Gatsby and then there was another silence.

`END`

The Finnish woman brought in the tea and we were glad to keep busy by passing around the cups and cakes. Daisy and I talked and Gatsby looked at us with unhappy eyes. After a while I stood up.

5   "Where are you going?" demanded Gatsby.

"I'll be back."

"I've got to speak to you about something before you go."

He followed me wildly into the kitchen, closed the door and whispered, "Oh, God!" in a miserable way.

"What's the matter?"

"This is a terrible mistake, a terrible mistake."

"You're just embarrassed, that's all," and luckily I added,

---

1.   **awkwardly** [ɔ:kwədli] : in an uncomfortable position.

"Daisy's embarrassed too."

"She's embarrassed?" he repeated.

"Just as much as you are."

"Don't talk so loud."

"You're acting like a little boy," I said impatiently. "Not only that, but you're rude. [1] Daisy's sitting in there all alone."

He raised his hand to stop my words, opened the door and went back to the other room.

I walked out the back way as Gatsby had done earlier and ran under a huge black tree, whose thick leaves protected me from the rain. Under the tree there was nothing to look at so I stared at Gatsby's enormous house.

6 After half an hour the sun shone again. I went back, after making every possible noise in the kitchen, but I don't think they heard a sound. They were sitting at either end of the couch looking at each other, and all embarrassment seemed to be gone. There were tears on Daisy's face and when I came in she jumped up and began drying her eyes in front of a mirror. But there was a change in Gatsby that was simply amazing— his great joy filled the small room.

"Oh, hello, old sport," he said, as if he hadn't seen me for years.

"It's stopped raining."

"Has it?" When he realized what I was talking about he smiled enthusiastically and repeated the news to Daisy.

"I want you and Daisy to come over to my house," he said. "I'd like to show her around."

---

1. **rude** : impolite.

Daisy went upstairs to wash her face, while Gatsby and I waited on the lawn.

"My house looks good, doesn't it," he demanded. "See how the whole front catches the light."

7 I agreed that it was splendid.

"Yes." His eyes looked at it carefully.

"It took me just three years to make the money that bought it."

"I thought you inherited the money."[1]

"I did, old sport, but I lost most of it during the war."

I think he hardly knew what he was saying, for when I asked him what business he was in he answered, "That's my affair," before he realized that it wasn't an appropriate reply.

"Oh, I've been in several things," he corrected himself. "I was in the drugstore business and then in the oil business. But I'm not in either one now."

Daisy then came out of the house.

"That huge place *there*?" she cried, pointing.

"Do you like it?"

"I love it! But how can you live there all alone?"

"I always keep it full of interesting people, night and day. Famous people."

Instead of just walking across the lawn we entered by the main gate. Daisy admired the huge structure and she admired the gardens with the sweet fragrance of the flowers.

8 Inside we walked through the grand rooms. We went upstairs through old-style bedrooms, dressing rooms and

---

1. **inherited the money** : received it after someone died.

luxurious [1] bathrooms. We went into one room where a young man was doing exercises on the floor. It was Mr Klipspringer, Gatsby's house guest. [2] Finally we came to Gatsby's own rooms—a bedroom, a bathroom and a study, where we sat down and drank a glass of liqueur.

He hadn't once stopped looking at Daisy and I think he gave a new value to everything in his house according to Daisy's reactions. Once he almost fell down some stairs.

His bedroom was the simplest room of all—except that on the dressing table there was a brush and comb set [3] of pure gold. Daisy took the brush with delight and smoothed her hair. Gatsby sat down and began to laugh. He had passed through two states and was entering a third. After his embarrassment and great joy he was now filled with wonder at her presence. It was a dream which he had dreamed for so long.

He opened two enormous cabinets which held his numerous suits, ties and shirts.

"I've got a man in England who buys my clothes. He sends over several things at the beginning of each season, spring and fall." [4]

He took out a pile of beautiful colored shirts and began throwing them one by one before us. Suddenly Daisy began crying wildly. "They're such beautiful shirts," she cried. "It makes me sad because I've never seen such beautiful shirts before."

---

1. **luxurious** : very fine and expensive.
2. **house guest** : a friend who lives at your house for a period of time.
3. **set** : two or more things with the same design.
4. **fall** : American term for autumn.

THE GREAT GATSBY

9 After the house, we were going to see the gardens and the swimming pool and the hydroplane and the flowers—but outside Gatsby's window it started raining again. We stood and looked at the misty[1] water.

"If it wasn't for the mist you could see your home across the bay," said Gatsby. "You always have a green light at the end of your dock."[2]

Daisy put her arm through his but he seemed absorbed[3] in what he had just said. Maybe he realized that the colossal significance of that light had now gone forever. Now that Daisy was next to him, it was again only a green light on the dock.

10 I walked around the room and saw a photograph of an elderly man in a yachting suit hanging over his desk.

"Who's this?" I asked.

"That's Mr Dan Cody, old sport. He's dead now. He used to be my best friend years ago."

"Come here, *quick!*" cried Daisy at the window.

The rain was still falling but there were pink and gold clouds in the West.

"Look at that," she whispered. "I'd like to get one of those pink clouds and put you in it and push you around."

I tried to go then, but they wouldn't let me.

11 "I know what we'll do," said Gatsby. "We'll ask Klipspringer to play the piano."

He went out of the room calling "Ewing!" and returned with

---

1. **misty** : foggy, hazy.

2. **dock** :

3. **absorbed** : concentrating completely.

the young man who looked embarrassed.

"I don't play well—I'm out of practice—"

"Let's go downstairs," said Gatsby.

In the music room Gatsby turned on a lamp beside the piano. He lit Daisy's cigarette with a shaking hand and sat down with her on a couch in a dark corner of the room.

After Klipspringer had played a song, he turned around unhappily and looked for Gatsby.

"I'm out of practice. I told you I couldn't play—"

"Don't talk so much, old sport," commanded Gatsby. "Play!"

12 Outside the wind was loud. All the lights were turning on in West Egg now. Men were returning from work. It was time for me to go home.

As I went to say goodbye I saw that an expression of uncertainty had returned to Gatsby's face. It seemed that he had a doubt about his present happiness. Almost five years had passed. There must have been moments that afternoon when Daisy had disappointed him, not because of her own fault but because of his colossal dream. What real person can equal a fantastic dream?

As I watched him his expression changed a little. His hand took hers and when she said something in his ear he turned toward her with great emotion. I think her voice was superior to all dreams.

They had forgotten about me, but Daisy looked up and held out her hand. Gatsby didn't know me at all now. They were possessed by intense vitality. I went out of the room and down the marble steps in the rain, leaving them there together.

The text and **beyond**

1 Comprehension check

Chapter Five has been divided into 12 sections. Choose the most suitable heading from the list below. There is one extra heading.

A ☐	A token of his appreciation		**G** ☐	An invitation to the castle
B ☐	A happy change in the weather		**H** ☐	Feeling out of place
C ☐	The king wishes to be amused		**I** ☐	A big mistake
			J ☐	A guided tour
D ☐	An awkward beginning		**K** ☐	Alone at last
E ☐	Finally she is really here		**L** ☐	Setting the date
F ☐	Singing in the rain		**M** ☐	Losing faith

2 Vocabulary – a crossword puzzle

Complete the puzzle below with words from the first five chapters.

Across

4 Nick came from a wealthy family and studied at Yale University. These are some of the ... that Nick had in life, and why his father says he shouldn't criticize other people. (10)

6 A person who cannot stay still is ... . This is the word that describes the wandering Buchanans. (8)

8 A long, narrow structure that goes out in the water. (Daisy had a green light at the end of hers.) (4)

9 A married man's lover. (8)

11 Certificates issued by a government or company promising that the money lent will be paid back with interest. (Nick's job is selling these.) (5)

14 Intoxicated. (Nick was in this state only twice in his life, and Daisy was in this state just before her wedding.) (5)

15 Brutal. (This word describes Tom's body.) (5)

17 What remains when something is burned. (A characteristic of the valley where Myrtle lives.) (5)

18 A person who tries to win money. (This is Mr Wolfshiem's occupation.) (7)

20 Move about without any particular goal or reason, pushed here and there by events. (This is how Daisy and Tom move about.) (5)

21 A pleasant and good-hearted person. (This seems to be Jay Gatsby's favorite word.) (5)

22 Foolish. (Gatsby feels like this when he gets upset because Daisy is a few minutes late.) (5)

23 If you are out of ..., it means that you have not done an activity (like playing the piano) for a long time. (8)

Down

1 An area of short, cut grass, often around houses. (4)

2 A town in the center of the United States, east of the Rocky Mountains, is a ... town. (10)

3 Extremely unhappy and distressed. (This word describes how Gatsby feels when he first meets Daisy.) (9)

5 American English for "petrol". (3)

7 Boats with an engine. (Gatsby had several of these which go up and down on the water in front of his beach.) (10)

10 A large house with land around it. (7)

12 American English for the British "chemist's", although in the United States they seem to sell just about everything. (9)

13 Anxiously. (This is how Daisy looked about when Tom left the room.) (8)

16 Bravery. (7)

19 A large, luxurious boat. (5)

Before you read

FCE ❶ **Gatsby's real background**

Read the passage below and decide which answer — A, B, C or D — best fits each space.

About this (0) ......D...... an ambitious young newspaper reporter from New York arrived at Gatsby's door and asked him if he had anything to say.

"Anything to say (1) .... what?" asked Gatsby politely.

"Why—any statement to give out."

It seemed that the reporter had (2) .... people talking about Gatsby and this could be a good story for the newspaper.

The reporter's instinct was right. Gatsby's notoriety was growing thanks to the hundreds of people who had attended his parties (3) .... the summer. They had created all sorts of legends about him that weren't true.

James Gatz was his (4) .... name and he came from North Dakota. His parents were poor, unsuccessful farm people and he had never really accepted them (5) .... his parents. He saw himself as a completely different person, who belonged to an extraordinary and beautiful world. At the age of seventeen he changed his name to Jay Gatsby and invented a new person with a new (6) .... and, hopefully, a brilliant future.

His new life began (7) .... he saw Dan Cody's yacht on Lake Superior. Cody was fifty years old then, and his gold and silver mines had made him (8) .... rich. He was physically strong but mentally weak. (9) .... women wanted his money, (10) .... Ella Kaye, a newspaper woman. He had been (11) .... on his yacht, the *Tuolomee*, (12) .... five years when he accidentally met James Gatz. James Gatz had been working on Lake Superior as a fisherman or doing (13) .... other job that brought him food and a bed.

84

As he was walking (**14**) .... the shore of Lake Superior one day
he saw Dan Cody's beautiful yacht stop in a dangerous area
(**15**) .... the shore. He borrowed a rowboat, went out to the
yacht and told its owner that a wind might destroy it in half an hour.

0	**A** moment	**B** instant	**C** hour	**D** time
1	**A** about	**B** for	**C** from	**D** of
2	**A** listened	**B** heard	**C** knew	**D** perceived
3	**A** for	**B** about	**C** during	**D** of
4	**A** valid	**B** real	**C** honest	**D** right
5	**A** as	**B** like	**C** for	**D** from
6	**A** identification	**B** individuality	**C** self	**D** identity
7	**A** as	**B** when	**C** while	**D** until
8	**A** much	**B** too	**C** very	**D** enough
9	**A** Lots	**B** Many	**C** Much	**D** Plenty
10	**A** including	**B** also	**C** covering	**D** plus
11	**A** journeying	**B** traveling	**C** voyaging	**D** going
12	**A** for	**B** since	**C** as	**D** from
13	**A** no	**B** every	**C** all	**D** any
14	**A** through	**B** along	**C** next	**D** up
15	**A** close	**B** next	**C** near	**D** vicinity

2 Nick Carraway is able to tell us about Gatsby's real background at this
point in the story because later on Gatsby tells Nick about himself.

What do you think Dan Cody will do after Gatsby (or Gatz as he was
then) has warned him about the danger to his boat? Write a sentence
with your prediction, and compare your sentences in class.

**Now read the beginning of Chapter Six to check your answers to
activity 1, and continue reading to check your predictions.**

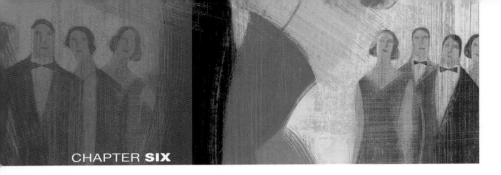

CHAPTER SIX

START **A**bout this time an ambitious young newspaper reporter from New York arrived at Gatsby's door and asked him if he had anything to say.

"Anything to say about what?" asked Gatsby politely.

"Why—any statement to give out."

It seemed that the reporter had heard people talking about Gatsby and this could be a good story for the newspaper.

The reporter's instinct was right. Gatsby's was becoming notorious [1] thanks to the hundreds of people who had attended his parties during the summer. They had created all sorts of legends about him that weren't true.

Gatsby himself told me the story very much later. James Gatz was his real name and he came from North Dakota. His parents were poor, unsuccessful farm people and he had never really accepted them as his parents. He saw himself as a completely different person, who belonged to an extraordinary and beautiful world. At the age of seventeen he changed his name to Jay Gatsby and invented a new person with a new identity and, hopefully, a brilliant future.

His new life began when he saw Dan Cody's yacht on Lake Superior. Cody was fifty years old then, and his gold and silver

---

1. **notorious** : well-known, but not well-known for a good reason.

mines had made him very rich. He was physically strong but mentally weak. Many women wanted his money, including Ella Kaye, a newspaper woman. He had been traveling on his yacht, the *Tuolomee*, for five years when he accidentally met James Gatz. James Gatz had been working on Lake Superior as a fisherman or doing any other job that brought him food and a bed.

As he was walking along the shore of Lake Superior one day he saw Dan Cody's beautiful yacht stop in a dangerous area near the shore. He borrowed a rowboat, [1] went out to the yacht and told its owner that a wind might destroy it in half an hour.

I suppose he smiled at Cody—he had probably discovered that people liked him when he smiled. Cody asked him a few questions and found that he was quick [2] and extremely ambitious. A few days later Cody bought him a blue coat, six pairs of white trousers and a sailor's cap. And when the *Tuolomee* left for the West Indies and the North African coast, Gatsby left too.

He worked as a sailor, a secretary and a cleaning man. He looked after Cody when he was drunk and irresponsible. This went on for five years and then one night Ella Kaye came on board the yacht and a week later Dan Cody died.

I remember the photograph of him in Gatsby's bedroom, a gray-looking man with a hard, empty face. He liked women and drinking—especially drinking. That was probably the reason Gatsby drank so little. And it was Cody who left him

1. **rowboat** :  2. **quick** : (here) clever.

money—twenty-five thousand dollars. Gatsby never got the money, and he never understood the legal strategies Ella Kaye used to inherit Cody's millions.

For several weeks after the tea party with Daisy I didn't see Gatsby. I was in New York most of the time going around with Jordan.

But finally one Sunday afternoon I went to Gatsby's house. I had only been there two minutes when someone brought Tom Buchanan in for a drink. I was surprised, of course, but the really surprising thing was that it hadn't happened before.

They were a party of three on horseback—Tom, a man named Sloane and a pretty woman who had been there before.

"I'm delighted to see you," said Gatsby standing on his porch. "Please sit down. I'll get you something to drink in just a minute."

Gatsby turned to Tom.

"I believe we've met before, Mr Buchanan."

"Oh, yes," said Tom politely, but obviously not remembering.

"About two weeks ago."

"Oh, that's right. You were with Nick."

"I know your wife," continued Gatsby almost aggressively.

"Is that so?"[1] Tom turned to me. "Do you live here, Nick?"

"Next door."

"Is that so?"

Tom was evidently worried that Daisy was going around alone, because on the following Saturday night he came with her to Gatsby's party. Perhaps Tom's presence gave the evening its strange quality of heaviness. I can still remember it. There were the same people, the same generous quantities of champagne, the same noise and the same activities, but I felt an unpleasantness in the air that hadn't been there before.

Tom and Daisy arrived at twilight[2] and we walked over to the colorful crowd.

"These things excite me so," she whispered to me.

"Look around," suggested Gatsby.

"I'm looking around. I'm having a marvelous—"

"You must see the faces of people you've heard about," Gatsby said.

Tom's arrogant eyes looked at the crowd.

"I don't know anyone here."

"Perhaps you know that lady." Gatsby indicated a beautiful

---

1. **Is that so?** : (colloquial expression) "Really?"
2. **twilight** : the period between sunset and darkness.

woman who sat under a tree. Tom and Daisy stared at her and recognized a famous movie actress.

"She's lovely," said Daisy.

"The man bending over her is her director."

He took them from group to group.

"Mrs Buchanan and Mr Buchanan—the polo player."

"I've never met so many famous people!" Daisy exclaimed.

"I'd rather not be called the 'polo player,'" said Tom.

Daisy and Gatsby danced. I had never seen him dance before and I was surprised by his graceful way of dancing. Then they went over to my house and sat on the steps for half an hour while, at her request, I remained in the garden. We returned to the party and as we were sitting down to supper, Tom appeared.

"Do you mind if I eat with some people over here?" he said.

"Go ahead," answered Daisy, "and if you want to write down any addresses, here's my little gold pencil."

She looked around and told me the girl with Tom was "common but pretty". I knew that except for the half hour she had been alone with Gatsby, she wasn't having a good time. Daisy didn't like the West Egg society. It offended her.

The people at our table were all rather drunk. Only two weeks before I had enjoyed these same people, but now they annoyed me.

I sat on the front steps near Daisy and Tom while they waited for their car.

"Who is this Gatsby?" demanded Tom suddenly. "Some big bootlegger?"

"Where did you hear that?" I asked.

"I didn't hear it, I guessed it. A lot of these newly rich people are just big bootleggers, you know."

"Not Gatsby," I said.

"Well, he certainly must have worked hard to get this strange collection of people together."

"At least they're more interesting than the people we know," said Daisy.

"You didn't look very interested."

"Well, I was," Daisy said and she started to sing with the music with her warm, magic voice.

"Lots of people come who haven't been invited," she said suddenly.

"I'd like to know who he is and what he does," Tom insisted. "And I'm going to find out."

"I can tell you right now," she answered. "He owned many drugstores. He built them up himself."

Their car came at last.

"Good night, Nick," said Daisy.

I stayed late that night. Gatsby asked me to stay until he was free. When he finally came down the stairs, he looked tired.

"She didn't like it," he said immediately.

"Of course she did."

"She didn't like it," he insisted. "She didn't have a good time."

He was silent and depressed.

"I feel far away from her," he said. "It's hard to make her understand."

"What do you mean?"

He told me that he wanted Daisy to say to Tom, "I never loved you". Then, when she was free, they could go back to

Louisville and get married— just as if it were five years ago.

"And she doesn't understand," he said. "She used to understand. We'd sit for hours—"

"You shouldn't ask too much of her," I said. "You can't repeat the past."

"Can't repeat the past?" he cried. "Of course you can! I'm going to arrange everything just the way it was before," he said with determination. "She'll see."

He talked a lot about the past and I realized that he wanted to get something back, perhaps an idea of himself that had gone into loving Daisy. His life had been confused and without order since then. But if he returned to a certain starting place, he could find out what the thing was...

One autumn night five years before, they had been walking down the street when the leaves were falling. They came to a place where there were no trees and the street was white with moonlight. They stopped here and turned toward each other.

His heart beat faster and faster as Daisy's white face came up to his own. He knew that when he kissed this girl he would lose some of his freedom. So he waited a moment longer, listening to the music of the stars. Then he kissed her. When his lips touched hers, she became a flower for him and the magic was complete.

The text and **beyond**

1 Comprehension check
Answer the following questions.

1 Why did Gatsby change his name?

2 How did Cody become rich?

3 What did Gatsby do for Dan Cody?

4 How did Ella Kaye become rich?

5 According to Nick, why did Tom come to Gatsby's party?

6 Why didn't Daisy have a good time at the party?

7 According to Tom, how did Gatsby become so wealthy?

8 According to Daisy, how did Gatsby become so wealthy?

9 What did Gatsby want to do with Daisy?

10 What do Nick and Gatsby disagree about?

2 Writing
You are Nick Carraway. Write a short letter to your father in which you explain who the "real" Jay Gatsby is, and why you find it difficult not to criticize Jay Gatsby, despite your father's advice.

Include in your letter:

- some of the stories about Gatsby
- why he has become the subject of so many stories
- what you think is the real origin of his wealth
- Gatsby's origins
- his friendship with Wolfshiem
- the real reason he gives such magnificent parties

You can begin like this:

Dear Father,

I know that you told me that whenever I feel like criticizing somebody I should remember that not everybody has had the advantages I have had. Well, my neighbor, Jay Gatsby, makes me wonder if your advice is always true.

Maybe you have heard of him. Certainly, there are many stories about him...

'I'd rather not be called the "polo player."'

Look at these sentences.

— *I'd rather not be called the "polo player"* ⇒ *I would rather not be called the "polo player"* ⇒ *I would prefer not to be called the "polo player".*

— *I'd rather go to the cinema* ⇒ *I would rather go to the cinema* = *I would prefer to go to the cinema.*

Notice that "I'd rather" is followed by the infinitive without "to", while "I'd prefer" is followed by the infinitive with "to".

3 **Expressing preferences**

For each question, use the elements to write one sentence with "would prefer" and one sentence with "would rather".

1 he/go/home/now

    ....

2 they/talk to you/directly

    ....

3 Tom/not meet/Jay

    ....

4 Jordan/not talk about Jay Gatsby

    ....

5 Jay Gatsby/see/Daisy

    ....

6 Nick/not drink too much

    ....

Before you read

1 **A declaration of love**

In Chapter Seven Tom will realize that Daisy loves Gatsby. How do you think that he will realize this?

1   Daisy will tell Tom, explicitly, that she has fallen in love with Gatsby.

2   Tom will notice Daisy looking at Gatsby in a special way.

3   Gatsby will ask to speak to Tom in private, and will tell him everything.

4   Tom will hear Gatsby and Daisy talking to each other.

Discuss your ideas in class before you read.

FCE **2** **Characters**

Read the beginning of Chapter Seven. For questions 1-9, identify the correct character (A-D). You can choose a letter more than once.

A Nick   **B** Daisy   **C** Gatsby   **D** Jordan

Which person

1   ☐   thinks Gatsby is sick?

2   ☐   fired all his/her servants?

3   ☐   thinks that Gatsby is leaving his house?

4   ☐   invites Nick to the Buchanans' for lunch?

5   ☐   is happy to hear Nick is coming to lunch?

6   ☐   can't move because of the heat?

7   ☐   laughs at Gatsby?

8   ☐   thinks that Tom is talking to his girlfriend on the phone?

9   ☐   thinks that Tom is pretending to talk to his girlfriend on the phone?

CHAPTER **SEVEN**

One Saturday night, when curiosity about Gatsby was at its highest, the lights at his house did not go on. The automobiles that turned into his driveway stayed for a minute, then drove sadly away. Wondering if he was sick, I went to his house. An unfamiliar butler with a criminal face opened the door.

"Is Mr Gatsby sick?"

"No." After a pause he unwillingly added "sir".

My Finnish cleaning woman informed me that Gatsby had fired [1] every servant in his house and replaced them with five or six others. The new servants ordered their supplies by phone and never went into West Egg village. The general opinion in the village was that the new people weren't servants at all.

The next day Gatsby called me on the phone.

"Going away?" I asked.

"No, old sport."

"I heard you fired all your servants."

"I wanted somebody who wouldn't gossip. [2] Daisy comes over quite often—in the afternoons. They're all people that Wolfshiem wanted to help. They're all brothers and sisters. They used to have a small hotel."

"I see."

---

1. **fired** : dismissed from work.
2. **gossip** : talk about other people's private lives.

He was phoning me at Daisy's request—would I come to the Buchanans for lunch tomorrow afternoon? Miss Baker would be there. Half an hour later Daisy herself phoned and seemed glad to know that I was coming. Something was going to happen.

The next day was very hot—the hottest day of the summer.

The Buchanans' living room was cool. Daisy and Jordan lay on the enormous couch in their white dresses.

"We can't move," they said together. Jordan's fingers rested in mine for a moment.

"And Mr Thomas Buchanan, the polo player?" I asked.

I heard his low voice in the hall, on the phone.

Gatsby stood in the middle of the room and looked around

with fascinated eyes. Daisy watched him and laughed her sweet, exciting laugh.

"It's probably Tom's girl on the phone," whispered Jordan.

We were silent. The voice in the hall was annoyed.

"Very well, then, I won't sell you the car at all... and don't bother me at lunch time!"

"Tom's not really talking into the phone," said Daisy.

"Yes, he is," I told her. "It's a real deal. [1] I know about it."

Tom opened the door and hurried into the room.

"Mr Gatsby!" He put out his broad, [2] flat hand with hidden dislike.

1. **deal** : (here) a business transaction.
2. **broad** : wide.

"I'm glad to see you, sir... Nick... "

"Make us a cold drink," said Daisy.

As he left the room again she got up and went over to Gatsby and pulled his face toward hers, kissing him on the mouth.

"You know I love you," she whispered.

At that moment a nurse came into the room with a little girl.

"My precious sweetheart," she cried, holding out her arms. "Come to your mother who loves you!"

The child rushed [1] across the room and hid her face in her mother's dress.

"My little dream! Stand up and shake hands."

Gatsby and I took the small hand. Afterward he kept looking at the child with surprise. I don't think he had ever really believed in its existence before.

"She doesn't look like her father," explained Daisy. "She looks like me."

Daisy sat back on the couch and the nurse took the child's hand and pulled her out of the room.

Tom came back with our icy drinks, which we drank eagerly.

"Come outside," he suggested to Gatsby. "I'd like you to have a look at the place."

I went out on the veranda [2] with them. Gatsby raised his hand and pointed across the bay.

"I'm right across from you."

---

1. **rushed** : moved very quickly.
2. **veranda** : like a porch, a covered area at the entrance.

"So you are."

We had lunch in the cool dining room.

"What'll we do with ourselves this afternoon?" cried Daisy. "And the day after that, and the next thirty years?"

"Life starts all over again when it's cool in the fall," said Jordan.

"But it's so hot," insisted Daisy, almost in tears. "And everything's so confused. Let's all go to town!"

Her voice struggled [1] against the heat.

"Who wants to go to town?" she demanded. Gatsby's eyes moved toward her.

"Ah," she cried, "you look so cool."

Their eyes met and they stared at each other. With an effort she looked down at the table.

"You always look so cool," she repeated.

She had told him that she loved him, and Tom Buchanan saw. His mouth opened a little, and he looked at Gatsby and then back at Daisy.

"You look like the man in that advertisement," she went on. "You know the advertisement of the man—"

"All right," interrupted Tom. "I'm willing to go to town. Come on—we're all going to town."

He got up, his eyes still flashing [2] between Gatsby and his wife. No one moved.

"Come on!" His anger was growing. "What's the matter? If we're going to town, let's start."

Daisy and Jordan went upstairs to get ready while we three

---

1. **struggled** : used a lot of physical effort and energy.
2. **flashing** : moving very rapidly.

men went outside in the heat.

"Shall we take anything to drink?" called Daisy from an upper window.

"I'll get some whiskey," said Tom as he went inside.

"I can't say anything in his house, old sport," said Gatsby.

"She's got a voice that gives away her feeling. It's full of—"

"Her voice is full of money," he said suddenly.

That was it. I'd never understood it before. It was full of money. That was the magic of her voice.

Tom came out of the house with a bottle wrapped [1] in a towel, followed by Daisy and Jordan.

"Shall we all go in my car?" suggested Gatsby.

"No, you take my car and I'll drive yours," said Tom.

Gatsby did not like the suggestion.

"I don't think there's much gas," he said.

"There's plenty of gas," said Tom. "And if it runs out I can stop at a drugstore. You can buy anything at a drugstore these days."

An unusual expression passed over Gatsby's face.

"Come on, Daisy," said Tom, pulling her toward Gatsby's car, but Daisy moved away.

"You take Nick and Jordan," she said. "We'll follow in your car."

Daisy walked close to Gatsby touching his coat with her hand.

Jordan and Tom and I got into the front seat of Gatsby's car, and we drove off into the oppressive heat.

---

1. **wrapped** : covered with paper or cloth.

"Did you see that?" demanded Tom.

"See what?"

He looked at me sharply,[1] realizing that Jordan and I must have known about Daisy and Gatsby.

"You think I'm rather stupid, don't you," he suggested. "Maybe I am, but I've made a small investigation into Gatsby's past."

"And you found he was an Oxford man," said Jordan.

"An Oxford man! Never! He wears a pink suit."

"Listen, Tom, why did you invite him to lunch, then?" asked Jordan angrily.

"Daisy invited him; she knew him before we were married— who knows where!"

We were all irritable now and drove in silence for a while. Then as Doctor T.J. Eckleburg's eyes came into sight, I remembered Gatsby's warning about the gas.

"We've got enough gas to get us to town," said Tom.

"But there's a garage right here," said Jordan.

Tom stopped the car impatiently under Wilson's sign. After a moment the owner came out and stared vacantly at the car.

"We want some gas!" cried Tom roughly.

"I'm sick," said Wilson, standing still. "I've been sick all day."

"Well, shall I help myself?" Tom asked. "You sounded well enough on the phone."

With an effort Wilson began to pump gasoline. In the sunlight his face was green.

---

1. **sharply** : intensely, severely.

"I didn't mean to interrupt your lunch," he said. "But I really need money now and I was wondering what you were going to do with your old car."

"Why do you suddenly need money?"

"I've been here too long. I want to get away. My wife and I want to get away. My wife and I want to go West."

"Your wife does!" cried Tom.

"She's been talking about it for ten years. And now she's going whether she wants to or not. I just found out that something strange has been going on and I want to take her away. That's why I've been bothering you about the car."

"What do I owe you?" [1]

"A dollar twenty."

The heat was beginning to confuse me but I realized that Wilson didn't suspect Tom yet. He had discovered that Myrtle had another life away from him in another world and the shock had made him sick. I looked at him and at Tom, who had made a similar discovery about an hour ago.

"I'll let you have that car tomorrow," said Tom.

Over the piles of ash the great eyes of Dr T.J. Eckleburg were watching us, but I saw that other eyes were watching us. In one of the windows over the garage the curtains had been moved to one side and Myrtle Wilson was looking at the car. Her eyes, wide with jealous terror, were staring at Jordan Baker, whom she thought was Tom's wife.

---

1. **What do I owe you?** : How much do I have to pay you?

The text and **beyond**

FCE **1** **Comprehension check**

For the following questions, choose the correct answer — A, B, C or D.

1 Why did the people drive away from Gatsby's after having stayed for just a moment?

A ☐ because there wasn't a party

B ☐ because he was sick

C ☐ because they didn't know the butler

D ☐ because they thought Gatsby was a bootlegger

2 Why did Gatsby fire all his servants?

A ☐ because he thought they might be criminals

B ☐ because he no longer needed them since he wasn't going to have any more big parties

C ☐ because they thought that he was a criminal

D ☐ because he didn't want anyone to talk about his relationship with Daisy

3 Who was Tom talking to on the phone?

A ☐ George Wilson

B ☐ Myrtle Wilson

C ☐ no one; he was just pretending to talk on the phone

D ☐ Wolfshiem

4 Why did Gatsby look at Daisy's daughter with surprise?

A ☐ because she was so beautiful

B ☐ because she looked so much like her mother

C ☐ because he hadn't thought that she actually existed

D ☐ because she looked so much like Tom

5 When did Tom discover that Daisy loved Gatsby?

A ☐ at one of Gatsby's parties

B ☐ the hot afternoon when Gatsby came to the Buchanans'

C ☐ when Daisy decided to drive to town with Gatsby

D ☐ when Gatsby told him

6 Why did Wilson want to take his wife away?

A ☐ because he thought they needed a rest

B ☐ because she was sick

C ☐ because he knew about her and Tom

D ☐ because he knew she had a secret life

2 Discussion

1 How does the weather in this chapter correspond to the mood of the characters?

2 Why do you think Gatsby's expression changes when Tom says, "You can buy anything at a drugstore these days."?

3 What does Tom mean when he says that Gatsby could not be an Oxford man because he wore a pink suit?

'... would I come to the Buchanans for lunch...'

Look at the direct questions and reported questions below. Observe how the word order and the tenses of the verbs change.

Also notice that if it is a yes/no question and there is no question word then "if" or "whether" is used in the reported question.

— *"What's the matter?" Tom asked.* ⇒ *Tom wanted to know what the matter was.*

— *"What are you doing?" Tom asked.* ⇒ *Tom asked what he was doing.*

— *"What do I owe you?" Tom enquired.* ⇒ *Tom wanted to know what he owed.*

— *"Have you seen her?" Daisy asked.* ⇒ *Daisy asked if he had ever seen her.*

— *"Did he go?" Nick asked.* ⇒ *Nick asked if had gone.*

— *"Will she come to your house?" Gatsby asked.* ⇒ *Gatsby asked if she would come to his house.*

— *"Are you going to ask her?" he asked Gatsby.* ⇒ *He asked whether Gatsby was going to ask her.*

3 Reporting questions

A **Turn the following direct questions into reported questions.**

1 "Why won't you help me?" the reporter asked Nick.

....

2 "Are they going to come over later?" Daisy asked.

....

3 "Where did you go?" Daisy asked Tom.

....

4 "Have you ever been to Montenegro?" Gatsby asked.

....

5 "Where did you go during the summer?" he asked.

....

6 "What will I do tomorrow and the next day and the next day?" Daisy asked.

....

B **Now turn the following reported questions into direct questions.**

1 She wanted to know what he was doing in her room.

....

2 He asked her why she never told the truth.

....

3 They asked where their car was.

....

4 I asked her whether she had eaten yet.

....

5 They asked me if I was going to Gatsby's party.

....

6 She asked me if I would wear my white linen suit.

....

Before you read

1 Reading pictures

Look at the picture on pages 114-115. In pairs or small groups, talk about what you can see and what you think has happened.

2 Tom and Gatsby

Read the first part of Chapter Eight and complete the following sentences with the missing information. You will need a word or a short phrase.

1   Tom was in a panic because he was no longer ....

2   When they got to New York, they began to ....

3   Daisy suffered greatly from the ....

4   Gatsby stayed at Oxford for ....

5   Gatsby had the opportunity to go to Oxford because he had been ....

6   Tom is very rude to ....

7   Gatsby told Tom that Daisy had never ....

8   According to Gatsby, Daisy didn't marry him because he was ....

START

There is no confusion like the confusion of a simple mind. And as we drove away Tom was in a panic. An hour ago he was sure about his wife and his girlfriend, but now they were slipping[1] out of his control.

We met Gatsby and Daisy and then we argued about how to spend the afternoon.

We finally decided to take out a suite at the Plaza Hotel. The suite was big and hot.

Daisy went to the mirror to look at her hair.

"Open another window," she commanded.

"There aren't any more," said Jordan.

"Well, we could make a hole in the wall—" said Daisy.

"Just forget about the heat," said Tom impatiently.

"Why don't you leave her alone, old sport," said Gatsby.

"That's a great expression of yours, isn't it?" said Tom.

"What is?"

"'Old sport'. Where did you pick it up?"

"Now listen, Tom," said Daisy, "if you're going to make personal remarks I won't stay here a minute. Order some drinks!"

Tom ordered the drinks and then suddenly said, "By the way, Mr Gatsby, I understand you're an Oxford man."

"Not exactly."

---

1. **slipping** : falling, moving.

"Oh, yes. I understand you went to Oxford."

"Yes, I went there."

"I'd like to know when," said Tom.

"It was in 1919. I only stayed five months. It was an opportunity given to some officers after the war. That's why I can't really call myself an Oxford man."

Daisy got up, smiling faintly, [1] and went to the table.

"Open the whiskey, Tom" she ordered.

"Wait a minute. I want to ask Mr Gatsby one more question."

"Go on," said Gatsby politely.

"What kind of trouble are you trying to cause in my house?"

They were out in the open at last, and Gatsby was glad.

"He isn't causing trouble," said Daisy. "You're causing trouble, Tom. Please have a little self-control."

"Self-control! I suppose I should let Mr Nobody from Nowhere make love to my wife."

"I've got something to tell *you*, old sport—," began Gatsby. "Your wife doesn't love you, do you hear? She's never loved you. She loves me."

"You must be crazy!" exclaimed Tom.

"She never loved you. She only married you because I was poor and she was tired of waiting for me. It was a terrible mistake, but in her heart she never loved anyone except me."

"Sit down, Daisy," said Tom. "What's been going on?"

"I told you what's been going on for five years," said Gatsby.

Tom turned to Daisy sharply, "You've been seeing this fellow for five years?"

---

1. **faintly** : weakly.

"Not seeing," said Gatsby. "No, we couldn't meet. But both of us loved each other all that time, old sport, and you didn't know."

"You're crazy!" he exploded. "Daisy loved me when she married me and she loves me now. And what's more, I love Daisy too. Once in a while I have an affair [1] but I always come back and in my heart I love her all the time."

"You're disgusting," said Daisy. She turned to me. "Do you know why we left Chicago? They haven't told you the story of that 'affair'?"

"Daisy, that's all over now," Gatsby said. "Tell him the truth that you never loved him."

She looked at him blindly.

"Why, how could I possibly love him?" she said.

"You never loved him."

Daisy hesitated. She looked at Jordan and at me as though she realized what she was doing—and that she had never intended doing anything at all. But it was done now. It was too late.

"I never loved him," she said reluctantly.

"Not on our wedding trip? Not on the day I carried you to keep your shoes dry?" There was tenderness in Tom's voice. "Daisy?"

"Please, don't," she said. She looked at Gatsby and tried to light a cigarette but her hand was shaking. Suddenly she threw the cigarette and the burning match on the carpet.

"Oh, you want too much," she cried to Gatsby. "I love you now—isn't that enough?" She began to cry. "I did love him once—but I loved you too."

---

1. **affair** : a sexual relationship with another woman.

"You loved me *too*?" Gatsby repeated.

"That's a lie," said Tom savagely. "She didn't know you were alive. There are things between Daisy and me that neither of us can forget."

The words seemed to bite physically into Gatsby.

"I want to speak to Daisy alone," he insisted.

"Even alone I can't say I never loved Tom. It wouldn't be true," she said.

"Of course, it wouldn't," agreed Tom. "And from now on I'm going to take better care of you."

"You don't understand," said Gatsby. "You're not going to take care of her any more."

"I'm not?" Tom opened his eyes wide and laughed. "Why?"

"Daisy's leaving you."

"Nonsense."

"I am, though," she said with a visible effort.

"She's not leaving me! Not for a common swindler [1] who goes around with Meyer Wolfshiem. I've been looking into your affairs! I found out what your 'drugstores' were." Tom turned to us. "He and Wolfshiem bought a lot of side-street drugstores here and in Chicago and they used them to sell alcohol. My friend Walter told me. But now you're on something much bigger—something Walter is afraid to tell me about."

The expression on Gatsby's face scared me, but after a moment it passed and he began to talk excitedly to Daisy. He denied [2] everything that had been said. But with every word she was drawing more and more into herself. Whatever courage and

---

1. **swindler** : someone who is false with people in order to make money.
2. **denied** : refused to say it was true.

whatever intentions she had had were definitely gone.

She asked again to go.

"Please Tom! I can't stand this [1] any more."

"You two go home, Daisy," said Tom. "In Mr Gatsby's car. Go on. He won't bother you now. He realizes it's over."

They went, without a word. After a moment Tom got up and began wrapping the unopened bottle of whiskey in the towel.

"Want any of this? Jordan? Nick?"

"No... I just remembered that today's my birthday."

I was thirty—the promise of loneliness in front of me. But there was Jordan beside me, who was wiser than Daisy. Her pale face fell lazily against my shoulder. So we drove on toward death in the cool twilight.

The young Greek, Michaelis, who owned the coffee shop beside the ash piles, was the principal witness of the accident. He told his story later at the investigation.

After five o'clock that afternoon he went over to the garage and found George Wilson sick in his office—really sick. Michaelis told him to go to bed but Wilson refused. They both heard a violent noise upstairs.

"I locked my wife in her room upstairs," explained Wilson calmly. "She's going to stay there until the day after tomorrow and then we're going to move away."

Michaelis was astonished. They had been neighbors for four years and Wilson had never seemed capable of such a thing. So Michaelis tried to find out what had happened, but Wilson wouldn't say a word. Instead, he began to question Michaelis, as

---

1. **I can't stand this** : it is impossible for me to be here.

though he suspected him. Michaelis was getting uneasy and went back to his coffee shop.

When he came outside again a little after seven, he heard Mrs Wilson's loud, angry voice in the garage.

A moment later she rushed out of the garage waving her hands and shouting.

The "death car", as the newspapers called it, didn't stop. It came out of the growing darkness, slowed down for a moment and then disappeared around the next bend. The other car, the one going toward New York, stopped and the driver hurried to where Myrtle Wilson lay dead on the road, her thick dark blood mixing with the dust.

We saw the cars and the crowd when we were still some distance away.

"A car crash!" said Tom. "Let's take a look." He stopped the car and we got out.

A deep, crying sound came from the garage.

"There's some bad trouble here," said Tom excitedly.

With his powerful arms he pushed his way through the crowd, while Jordan and I followed.

Myrtle Wilson's body was wrapped in a blanket and lay on a work table.

Tom bent over it, motionless. A policeman stood next to him, writing down names. Then I saw Wilson standing in the doorway of his office, moving back and forth and giving out a horrible call.

"Oh my God! Oh my God! Oh my God!"

Tom asked the policeman, "What happened—that's what I want to know."

"Car hit her. Killed instantly. She ran out into the road. The driver didn't even stop his car."

"It was a yellow car," said a well-dressed black man. "Big new yellow car."

Wilson evidently heard this.

"You don't have to tell me what kind of car it was. I know what kind of car it was," said Wilson.

Tom walked over to Wilson and helped him to stand up.

"Listen," said Tom nervously. "I just got here from New York. I was bringing you that car we've been talking about. That yellow car I was driving this afternoon wasn't mine, do you hear?"

Tom picked up Wilson like a doll and carried him into the office.

"Can someone come here and sit with him?" he said. Two men went unwillingly into the room.

"Let's get out," Tom whispered to me.

Tom's car raced through the night as tears ran down his face.

"The dirty coward! He didn't even stop his car."

The Buchanans' house suddenly appeared through the dark trees. Tom looked up at Daisy's windows on the second floor.

"Daisy's home," he said. "I should have left you in West Egg, Nick. I'll phone for a taxi to take you home and while you're waiting you and Jordan can have some supper in the kitchen—if you want it."

"No, thanks. I'll just wait for the taxi outside."

Jordan put her hand on my arm.

"Are you coming in, Nick?"

"No thanks."

I was feeling a little sick and I wanted to be alone. I'd had enough of all of them for one day and suddenly that included Jordan too. She probably understood this because she turned away and went into the house.

Suddenly I heard my name and Gatsby walked out of the darkness in his pink suit.

"What are you doing?" I asked.

"Just standing here, old sport."

After a minute he asked, "Did you see any trouble on the road?"

"Yes."

He hesitated.

"Was she killed?"

"Yes."

"I thought so. I told Daisy I thought so. It's better if the shock comes all at once. She took it rather well."

He spoke as if Daisy's reaction was all that mattered. [1]

"I got to West Egg by the side road and left my car in my garage. I don't think anybody saw us."

I disliked him so much by this time that I didn't tell him he was wrong.

"Who was the woman?" he asked.

"Her name was Wilson. Her husband owns the garage. How did it happen?"

"Well, I tried to swing the wheel—"

Suddenly I guessed the truth.

"Was Daisy driving?"

"Yes," he said after a moment, "but of course I'll say I was

---

1. **mattered** : was important.

driving. When we left New York she was very nervous and she thought that driving would calm her. The woman ran out at us just as we were passing a car coming from the other direction. It all happened in a minute but it seemed to me that she wanted to speak to us. Well, first Daisy turned away from the woman toward the other car, and then she was afraid and turned back. When my hand touched the wheel I felt the shock—it must have killed her instantly. I tried to make Daisy stop but she couldn't.

"She'll be all right tomorrow," he continued. "I'm just going to wait here and see if he tries to bother her."

"He won't touch her. He's not thinking about *her*. How long are you going to wait?"

"All night if necessary. Well, until they go to bed," Gatsby said.

A new thought occurred to me. Suppose Tom found out that Daisy had been driving. He might see a connection in it.

"You wait here," I said. "I'll see if there's any sign of trouble."

I walked silently to the house. From the kitchen window I could see Daisy and Tom sitting opposite each other at the table.

They weren't happy and yet they weren't unhappy either. They seemed to be planning something together.

"It's all quiet up there. Come home and get some sleep."

He shook his head.

"I'll wait here until Daisy goes to bed. Good night, old sport." He turned back to look at the house and I walked away leaving him there in the moonlight—watching over nothing.

The text and **beyond**

1 Comprehension check

**Number the sentences in the right order to make a summary of
Chapter Eight.**

A ☐ When they arrived at the Buchanans' house, Jordan and Tom
went inside, and Nick waited outside for a taxi. Suddenly,
Gatsby appeared out of the darkness.

B ☐ As they were driving past Wilson's gas station, Myrtle ran out
into the road and Daisy hit her, but she did not stop the car.

C ☐ He then went home, and Gatsby stayed to watch over nothing.

D ☐ Tom began to ask Gatsby about his love affair with Daisy and
to accuse Gatsby of being a criminal.

E ☐ A little later Tom, Nick and Jordan arrived at the gas station
and a policeman told Tom that Myrtle had been hit by a big
yellow car.

F ☐ Daisy ended up driving because she thought driving would
calm her down.

G ☐ He then drove home, thinking what a coward Gatsby was for
not even stopping.

H ☐ Tom, Daisy, Nick and Jordan rented a suite in a hotel.

I ☐ Talking with him, Nick realized for the first time that Daisy
had been driving the car.

J ☐ Daisy became frightened and asked Tom to take her home, but
Tom told her to go with Gatsby.

2 Discussion

1 What does Nick mean when he says that Daisy looked at him "as
though she realized what she was doing—and that she had never
intended doing anything at all"?

2 Nick says that Tom and Daisy "seemed to be planning something
together". What do you think they were planning?

3 What does Nick mean when he says that he left Gatsby "watching
over nothing"?

3 Speaking

The Wilsons live in the Valley of Ashes, far from the glamour of Manhattan or East Egg. They are also, in a sense, far from the reader, because the narrator, Nick, knows much less about them than he does about Tom, Daisy or Gatsby. As a result, he doesn't tell us very much about them, and so the Wilsons remain both at the edge of society and at the edge of the story.

In pairs or small groups, imagine their lives, and invent their story, the details which the novel doesn't tell us. Talk about

- where and when they were born
- what their parents were like
- what kind of education they had
- when and where they met each other
- why they got married, and what the marriage and honeymoon were like
- what their married life together was like
- other details that occur to you

FCE 4 Writing

You are Myrtle and you are locked up in your room. You are writing a letter to your best friend, Louise, just before your tragic death. In this letter explain why you are in the room.

Include the following information:

- how you met Tom
- why you decided to become his lover
- what he did for you
- what your husband did when he discovered you had a lover
- what you thought when you saw Tom drive up to the garage with Nick and Jordan

Write between 120-180 words. Finish your letter like this:

I can see Tom coming round the corner in that big yellow car he was driving before. I'll just go and stop him. I will write you another letter tomorrow.

Your friend forever,
Myrtle

American Literature in the 1920s

The 1920s were a fertile period for American literature. The many social, economic and cultural changes brought on a burst [1] of creativity with literary talents such as Fitzgerald, Hemingway, Dos Passos, Wharton, Sinclair Lewis and Faulkner. Although their writing styles and subject matters were quite different, these writers became social historians of their times. They portrayed the part of society which they knew best and the events which affected people's lives.

After World War I, many writers and poets were attracted to Paris, which was then a center of literary development. Here, writers and poets could work in a cultural and liberal atmosphere. One of these was Ernest Hemingway, who was among the first American writers to use a colloquial, journalistic writing style.

Hemingway's first novel, *The Sun Also Rises* (*Fiesta* in Britain) published in 1926, was very different from previous American fiction. Although it was an innovative work, it met with great success and brought him fame. The novel describes the lives of American and British expatriates [2] who travel between Paris and Spain, leading decadent, nonconformist lives. His second novel, *A Farewell to Arms* (1929), based in part on his personal experiences as an ambulance driver in Italy during World War I, was an immediate success. During his adventurous and exciting life Hemingway

1. **burst** : explosion.
2. **expatriates** : people living in a foreign country.

became one of the most famous writers of his generation. Some of his other well-known works include collections of short stories, and the novels *For Whom the Bell Tolls* and *The Old Man and the Sea*, for which he received the Pulitzer Prize. In 1954 he was awarded the Nobel Prize for literature.

While in Paris Hemingway met John Dos Passos, another American writer who had served in World War I, and they became good friends. His novel *Three Soldiers* (1921) was one of the first works to condemn [1] the horrors and futility [2] of war. Dos

Edith Wharton (1862-1937)

Passos became involved in experimental drama and also published a political magazine in the United States. *Manhattan Transfer* (1925) and *U.S.A.* (1937) were John Dos Passos's most important works. His literary career continued right up to his death in 1970.

Edith Wharton was another outstanding American writer who spent many years in Europe. Wharton grew up in a rich New York family and in her novels she revealed the snobbery [3] and hypocrisy of New York's high society. Although Edith Wharton was of an

1. **condemn** : denounce, disapprove.
2. **futility** : uselessness.
3. **snobbery** : arrogance, superior attitude.

earlier generation, she published her masterpiece, *The Age of Innocence*, in 1920 and was the first woman to receive the Pulitzer Prize. Some of her other works include *The House of Mirth, Ethan Frome* and *Xingu and Other Stories*.

While Fitzgerald portrayed the Jazz Age, Sinclair Lewis wrote his satirical attacks on the society of the American Midwest. He ridiculed the narrow-minded [1] mentality of provincial America with his novels *Main Street* (1920) and *Babbitt* (1922). His works exposed "another America"—where conformity, prejudice, ignorance and money were the protagonists. In 1926 Sinclair Lewis was awarded

William Faulkner
(1897-1962)

the Pulitzer Prize, which he refused. Four years later he became the first American to be awarded the Nobel Prize for Literature, which he accepted. Lewis realized the importance of the Nobel Prize because it brought prestige and recognition to American writers.

Late in the 1920s William Faulkner, another promising [2] writer, started experimenting with different narrative techniques. The result of this experiment was his masterpiece, *The Sound and the Fury* (1929), where different characters narrate different parts of the story. Since his first

1. **narrow-minded** : prejudiced, considering only part of a question, favoring only one opinion.
2. **promising** : showing signs of future success.

novels were innovative and were concerned with controversial topics such as murder, mental illness, religion and interracial [1] relationships they did not have much success. Faulkner was from the South (the state of Mississippi) and he was deeply concerned about decadent southern society. In order to earn money he periodically worked as a scriptwriter in Hollywood for twenty years, and wrote the scripts for many important films, such as *The Big Sleep* (1946). In the 1940s critics began to understand and appreciate Faulkner, and in 1949 he received the Nobel Prize for literature. Some of his best works include *As I Lay Dying, Sanctuary, Go Down Moses* and *Absalom, Absalom!*

The years that followed produced many other talented American writers, but the 1920s will always be remembered as the turning point [2] of American literature at an international level.

1 Comprehension check
Answer the following questions.

1 What was Hemingway's writing style like?
2 What was *The Sun Also Rises* about?
3 Describe Don Passos's literary career.
4 What did Edith Wharton write about?
5 What did Sinclair Lewis write about?
6 Which major literary award did Sinclair Lewis refuse?
7 Which major literary award did he accept, and why?
8 Why weren't Faulkner's works very successful when they first came out?
9 Which commercial activity did Faulkner do to earn a living?

---

1. **interracial** : between two races.
2. **turning point** : point in time when a very important change takes place.

125

FCE ❷ Fill in the gaps

For questions 1-12, read the text below and think of the word which best fits each gap. Use only one word in each gap. There is an example at the beginning (0).

The Life of Ernest Hemingway

Fitzgerald and Hemingway, just three years younger than Fitzgerald, are the two most famous American writers (**0**)...*of*.... the 20th century. Their fame does not depend entirely (**1**)......... the quality of their writing: their lifestyles also played a big part (**2**)......... creating their reputations. Hemingway was famous (**3**)......... his adventurous lifestyle — and his four marriages — even during his (**4**)......... lifetime. During Word War I he served (**5**)......... an ambulance driver for the American Red Cross: he was wounded (**6**)......... serving in northern Italy and was awarded a medal for bravery. After the war, he took (**7**)......... a career as foreign correspondent for North American newspapers. Based in Paris, he traveled widely for the skiing, bullfighting, hunting and fishing (**8**)......... by then were the background for much of his fiction. Acting as a war reporter, Hemingway (**9**)......... four trips to Spain during the Spanish Civil War (1936-39) and raised money for the Republicans. The war provided the background to his novel *For Whom the Bell Tolls*, which sold many (**10**)......... copies than his other books. Hemingway was at the height of his fame after the book came (**11**)......... in 1940, the year Fitzgerald died. After reporting World War II in Europe he went to live in Cuba. But in (**12**)......... of winning the Pulitzer and Nobel prizes, he suffered from depression, alcoholism and a fear that he was losing his ability to write, and he committed suicide in 1961.

Before you read

❶ What happens next?

At the end of Chapter Nine two people will be dead. Who, do you think? How will they have died?

CHAPTER **NINE**

I couldn't sleep all night. I was half sick between grotesque reality and frightening dreams. Towards dawn [1] I heard a taxi go up to Gatsby's house and I immediately jumped out of bed and began to dress. I had to warn him about something and morning would be too late.

Crossing his lawn I saw that his front door was still open.

"Nothing happened," he said. "I waited and at about four o'clock she came to the window and turned off the light."

His house had never seemed so enormous to me as it did that night.

"You ought to go away," I said. "They'll surely find your car."

"Go away now, old sport?"

He wouldn't consider it. He couldn't possibly leave Daisy until he knew what she was going to do. He was holding on to a last hope and I couldn't tell him that there was no hope.

It was this night that he told me the strange story of his youth with Dan Cody. He told me because "Jay Gatsby" had broken up like glass against Tom's malice, and the extravagant show was finished.

He wanted to talk about Daisy. She was the first "nice" girl he had ever known. He found her extremely desirable. He went to her house at first with other Army officers and then alone. Her house amazed him—he had never been in such a

1. **dawn** : the first light in the sky before the sun rises.

beautiful house before. It had an air of romance and mystery because Daisy lived there.

But he knew that he was in Daisy's house by accident. He took what he could get and one October night he took her. He had let her believe that he came from the same social background, and was fully capable of taking care of her. But he had no comfortable family standing behind him—he was penniless. [1] He had probably intended to take what he could and go—but now he realized that he was deeply tied to Daisy. He knew Daisy was extraordinary but he didn't realize how extraordinary a "nice" girl could be. She disappeared into her rich house leaving Gatsby with nothing. He felt married to her, that was all.

"I can't tell you how surprised I was to find out I loved her. I even hoped for a while that she would leave me, but she was in love with me too. She thought I knew a lot because I knew different things from her... Well, I was far from my ambitions and falling in love deeper every minute."

On the last afternoon before he went to war he sat with Daisy in his arms for a long, silent time. It was a cold, fall day with a fire in the room. That afternoon had made them ready for the long separation that was to come. They had never been closer in their month of love.

He did extraordinarily well in the war. He became a captain before going to fight in France. After the war he tried very hard to return home, but he was sent to Oxford instead. He was worried by Daisy's letters, which had a quality of nervous

---

1. **penniless** : without any money.

despair. She wanted him to return and feel him beside her. She wanted to be sure she was doing the right thing.

Daisy was young and she felt the pressure of her artificial world, filled with music, dances and flowers. She began to move again with the season and to accept invitations from different young men. She desperately wanted to make a decision about her life, and Tom Buchanan arrived at the right moment. There was a certain solidity [1] about his person and his position, and Daisy decided to put her future in his hands. The letter reached Gatsby while he was still at Oxford.

It was dawn on Long Island now and we opened the windows of the house.

"I don't think she ever loved him." Gatsby looked at me. "Remember, old sport, she was very excited this afternoon and didn't know what she was saying. Of course, she might have loved him for a minute, when they were first married— and she loved me even more then, do you see?"

He had come back from France when Tom and Daisy were still on their wedding trip and made a miserable trip to Louisville on his last Army pay. He stayed there a week, walking the streets where they had walked together. He was penniless when he left on the bus.

It was nine o'clock when we had finished breakfast. The gardener came to the foot of the steps.

"I'm going to empty the pool today, Mr Gatsby."

"Don't do it today."

Gatsby turned to me and said, "You know, I haven't used the pool all summer."

---

1. **solidity** : the quality of being solid, stable.

I looked at my watch and stood up.

"Twelve minutes to my train."

I didn't want to go to the city. I didn't feel like working, but it was more than that—I didn't want to leave Gatsby. I missed that train and then another before I went away.

"I'll call you at about noon," I said finally.

"Do, old sport."

We walked down the steps.

"I suppose Daisy'll call too." He looked at me anxiously.

"I suppose so."

"Well, goodbye."

We shook hands and I walked away. Just before reaching my garden I remembered something and turned around.

"They're a rotten [1] crowd," I shouted. "You're worth the whole bunch of them!"

I've always been glad I said that. It was the only compliment I ever gave him, because I disapproved of him from beginning to end. First he nodded [2] politely, and then he smiled his wonderful, radiant smile.

"Goodbye," I called. "I enjoyed breakfast, Gatsby."

In the city I tried to work but I fell asleep. Just before noon Jordan Baker phoned me. Usually her voice was fresh and cool, but this morning it wasn't. We talked for a while and then suddenly we weren't talking anymore. I don't know who hung up [3] but I know I didn't care.

I then called Gatsby's house but the line was busy. I took

---

1. **rotten** : (here) bad, nasty.
2. **nodded** : moved his head up and down to express agreement.
3. **hung up** : put down the telephone, ended the conversation.

out my timetable [1] and drew a circle around the three-fifty train. It was just noon.

Now I want to go back a little and talk about what happened at the garage after we left there the night before.

Michaelis had stayed with Wilson all night long. About three o'clock that morning Wilson became quieter and began talking about the yellow car.

"The man in the yellow car murdered her. She ran out to speak to him and he didn't stop."

He said that he had a way of finding out who the yellow car belonged to. Then he said that a few months ago his wife had come from the city with a broken nose.

"Yesterday afternoon I found this." He pulled out a new, expensive dog leash [2] from the drawer. "She tried to tell me about it but I knew she was lying—I knew she had another man. I took her to the window and said she could fool [3] me but she couldn't fool God."

With an effort he got up and walked to the rear window. "God sees everything."

Michaelis saw with a shock that he was looking at the enormous eyes of Doctor T.J. Eckleburg.

"That's an advertisement," Michaelis said.

By six o'clock Wilson was calmer and Michaelis went home to sleep, but when he woke up four hours later and went back

---

1. **timetable** : a piece of paper showing train times.
2. **dog leash** :
3. **fool** : (here) deceive, trick.

to the garage, Wilson was gone.

Wilson was on foot all the time and there were boys who had seen a man "acting sort of crazy". [1] For three hours he disappeared. The police thought he spent the time going from garage to garage asking about a yellow car. By half past two he was in West Egg, where he asked someone the way to Gatsby's house. So by that time he knew Gatsby's name.

At two o'clock Gatsby put on his bathing suit and told his butler to advise him if anyone phoned. He went to the garage to get a water mattress and then gave instructions—the yellow car must not be taken out for any reason.

Gatsby started for the pool with the water mattress. No phone call arrived. The butler waited for it until four o'clock. I think Gatsby himself didn't believe the call from Daisy would arrive and perhaps he didn't care any more.

The driver heard the shots but he later said that he hadn't thought much about them. I drove from the station directly to Gatsby's house and rushed up the front steps. The driver, the butler the gardener and I hurried down to the pool.

The mattress with its burden [2] moved down the pool, leaving a red trail [3] in the water.

After we started carrying Gatsby to the house, the gardener saw Wilson's body in the grass and the tragedy was complete.

---

1. **acting sort of crazy** : behaving in a very strange way.
2. **burden** : load (here, Gatsby's body).
3. **trail** : marks.

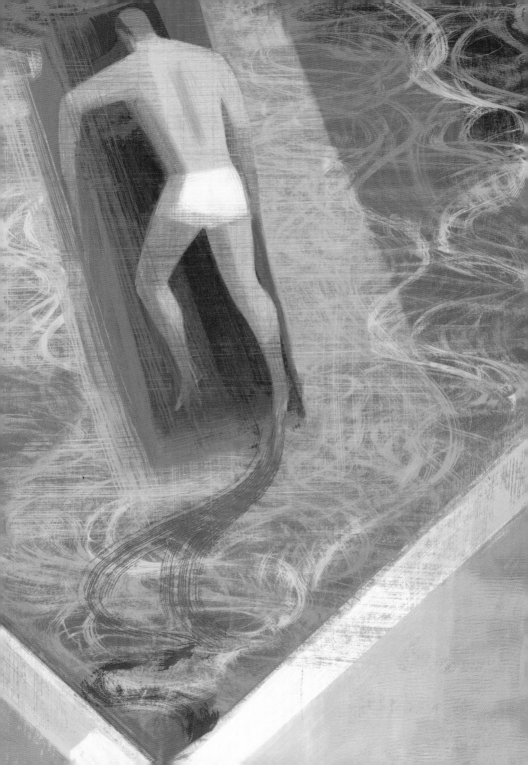

The text and **beyond**

1 **Comprehension check**
Answer the following questions.

1   Why didn't Gatsby take Nick's advice and go away?

2   Why was Gatsby so amazed by Daisy's house?

3   How did Gatsby deceive Daisy?

4   How did Gatsby do during the war?

5   Why did Daisy begin going out with other young men?

6   Why did Daisy decide to marry Tom?

7   In what condition was Gatsby when he returned to Louisville after the war?

8   What was the compliment that Nick paid to Gatsby?

9   Why was it the only compliment that he ever paid to him?

10 How did Wilson discover that his wife was seeing another man?

11 Why did Wilson kill Gatsby?

12 What happened to Wilson in the end?

FCE **2** **Word formation**
Read the text below. Use the word given in capitals at the end of the lines to form a word that fits in the space in the same line. There is an example at the beginning (0).

Public Enemy Number One

F. Scott Fitzgerald in his short novel *The Great Gatsby* presents a (**0**) .....striking..... picture of gangsters in the	STRIKE
characters of Gatsby and Wolfshiem. In real life the symbol of (**1**) .... businessmen was Al	LEGAL
Capone. Al Capone was born on January 17, 1899 in Brooklyn, New York. He did well in school, but he was more interested in the "kid gangs" of his	
(**2**)	NEIGHBOR
As a young man he worked for various (**3**)	GANG
and in 1918 he committed his first two murders.	

134

In 1919 Capone went to Chicago where he worked for the bootlegger John Torrios.

Torrios appreciated Capone's intelligence and (4) .... In 1925 Torrios was forced to leave Chicago and so Capone took over. He proved to be an extremely (5) .... crime boss and expanded the business so that it soon had (6) .... of $100,000,000 every year. Capone was (7) .... for the notorious Saint Valentine's Day Massacre, which eliminated the gang of a rival bootlegger. This gangland killing became a (8) .... newspaper story. Capone, as always, had the perfect alibi: he was in Florida on Saint Valentine's Day. However, Al Capone was (9) .... sent to prison for tax evasion. Capone was eventually released and he spent his last years living (10) .... at his home in Florida, where he died on January 21, 1947.

BRAVE

ABILITY
EARN

RESPONSE

SENSATION

FINAL

PEACE

Before you read

FCE **1** **After the death**

Read the first part of Chapter Ten. For questions 1-7, choose the best answer — A, B, C or D — for the following questions.

1 How does Nick remember the two days after Gatsby's death?

   A ☐ as being grotesque

   B ☐ as crazy

   C ☐ as full of police and photographers

   D ☐ as a bad dream

2 What did Myrtle's sister, Catherine, say during the investigation?

   A ☐ Myrtle and Tom were lovers.

   B ☐ Gatsby was Myrtle's lover.

   C ☐ Myrtle was happy with her husband and had no lover.

   D ☐ She hardly knew her sister.

3 What did the investigation decide about Myrtle's death?

A ☐ Her lover had killed her.

B ☐ Daisy had killed her by accident.

C ☐ A stranger had killed her by accident.

D ☐ Wilson had shot his wife's lover.

4 Why was Nick responsible for Gatsby after his death?

A ☐ because nobody else cared about him

B ☐ because he was his closest friend

C ☐ because Daisy couldn't come

D ☐ because he had made a promise to Gatsby

5 What did Slagle want to tell Gatsby about Parke?

A ☐ He had gone away without leaving an address.

B ☐ He was in Chicago.

C ☐ The police had caught him.

D ☐ He had been buying stolen bonds.

6 Who was Henry C. Gatz?

A ☐ Gatsby's father

B ☐ a reporter from Chicago

C ☐ a young man arrested because he was selling stolen bonds

D ☐ Gatsby's older brother

7 How did Gatz find out about Gatsby's death?

A ☐ The police told him.

B ☐ Tom sent him a telegram.

C ☐ Daisy phoned him.

D ☐ He read about it in the newspaper.

2 Reading pictures

Look at the picture on pages 142-44. Who do you think the people are?

START

After two years I remember the rest of that day and that night and the next day as an endless procession of police, photographers and newspapermen in and out of Gatsby's front door. A detective used the word "crazy" as he looked at Wilson's body and the newspaper reports the next morning followed this idea. Most of the reports were grotesque and untrue.

At the investigation Michaelis revealed that Wilson suspected that his wife was seeing another man. Catherine, who might have said anything, didn't say a word. She showed a surprising strength of character. She swore [1] that her sister had never seen Gatsby and that she was completely happy with her husband. So the investigation decided that Myrtle Wilson had been accidentally killed by a stranger and George Wilson, who was mad with grief, [2] shot him and then shot himself.

As Gatsby lay in his house and didn't move or breathe or speak I realized that I was responsible because no one else was interested. I found myself on Gatsby's side.

I phoned Daisy half an hour after we found him, but she and Tom had already gone with their baggage and had left no address.

I wanted to get somebody for him. I wanted to go into the

---

1. **swore** : *(swear - swore - sworn)* declared something to the police.
2. **grief** : great suffering and sadness.

room where he lay and reassure him: "I'll get somebody for you, Gatsby. Don't worry. Just trust me."

I tried to call Meyer Wolfshiem but he wasn't in. I went upstairs and looked through the unlocked parts of his desk. He had never told me definitely that his parents were dead. But there was nothing, only the picture of Dan Cody on the wall.

The next morning I sent the butler to New York with a letter to Wolfshiem asking him to come on the next train. I was sure he would come when he saw the newspapers, just as I was sure Daisy would send a telegram before noon. But neither arrived.

The butler brought back Wolfshiem's answer:

> Dear Mr Carraway,
> This has been a terrible shock for me. But I cannot come down now as I am tied up in some very important business and cannot get involved in this thing.
>
> Yours truly,
> Meyer Wolfshiem

When the phone rang that afternoon from Chicago I thought it would be Daisy at last. But it was a man's voice on the phone.

"This is Slagle speaking..."

"Yes?" I didn't know the name.

"Young Parke's in trouble," he said. "The police caught him when he tried to sell those stolen bonds."

"Look! This isn't Mr Gatsby. Mr Gatsby is dead."

There was a long silence followed by an exclamation... then

suddenly the man hung up.

I think it was on the third day that a telegram signed Henry C. Gatz arrived from a town in Minnesota. It said that he was leaving immediately and to postpone the funeral until his arrival.

It was Gatsby's father, a solemn, helpless old man. He was in a very sad state.

"I saw it in the Chicago newspaper," he said. "I came right away."

END

"I didn't know how to reach you."

His eyes moved about the room.

"It was a madman. He must have been mad."

"Wouldn't you like some coffee?" I asked.

"I don't want anything. Where is Jimmy?"

I took him into the room where his son lay and left him there.

After a while Mr Gatz opened the door and came out, his mouth open and a few tears on his face. He had reached an age where death was no longer a terrible surprise. When he looked around for the first time and saw the splendor of the hall and the great rooms, his grief was mixed with pride. I took him to a bedroom upstairs and told him that the funeral had been postponed until he came.

"I didn't know what you'd want, Mr Gatsby—"

"Gatz is my name."

"Mr Gatz, I thought you might want to take the body back to the West."

He shook his head. "Jimmy always liked the East better. He rose up to his position in the East. If he'd lived he would have been a great man. He would have helped build the country."

"That's true," I said uncomfortably.

He lay down on the bed and fell asleep immediately.

That night I received a call from Klipspringer, who had been Gatsby's houseguest for a long time.

"The funeral's tomorrow," I said. "Three o'clock at the house. I wish you'd tell anyone who'd be interested." I didn't want to put it in the newspapers and draw curious crowds, so I'd been calling a few people myself. They were hard to find.

"Of course, you'll be there yourself," I said.

"Well, I don't know... but what I called about was a pair of tennis shoes I left there. Could you ask your butler to send them to me? My address is—"

I didn't hear the address because I hung up in disgust.

The morning of the funeral I went up to New York to see Meyer Wolfshiem. At first there didn't seem to be anyone in the office, but after having shouted "hello" many times, Meyer appeared.

"This is a sad time for all of us," he said. "My memory goes back to the first time I met him. He was just out of the army and he was so poor he had only his army uniform. He hadn't eaten anything for a couple of days. I invited him to lunch and he ate more than four dollars' worth of food in half an hour."

"Did you start him in business?" I asked.

"Start him! I made him. I raised him up out of nothing. I saw that he was a gentleman and when he told me he went to Oxford I knew I could use him. He did some work for a friend of mine right away. We were like that,"—he held up two fat fingers—"always together."

"Now he's dead," I said. "You were his closest friend so I know you'll want to come to the funeral this afternoon."

He shook his head and his eyes filled with tears.

"I can't do it—I can't get mixed up in it. When a man gets killed I never get mixed up in it. Let us learn to show our friendship for a man when he is alive and not after he is dead," he said.

I returned to West Egg, changed my clothes and went next door. I found Mr Gatz walking excitedly up and down the hall. His pride in his son and in his son's possessions was increasing.

"Had you seen your son recently?" I asked.

"He came out to see me two years ago and bought me the house I live in now. Ever since he had success he was very generous with me."

A little before three the minister arrived from the church and I began to look out of the window for other cars. So did Gatsby's father. The servants came in and we all stood waiting in the hall. I asked the minister to wait for half an hour. But it wasn't any use. Nobody came.

About five o'clock our procession of three cars reached the cemetery and stopped beside the gate. It was raining. As we entered the cemetery I heard a car stop and I looked around. It was the man with the enormous round glasses whom I had found in Gatsby's library three months before. The rain poured down [1] on his thick glasses, and he took them off and cleaned them to see Gatsby being put into his grave. [2]

---

1. **poured down** : came down very heavily.
2. **grave** : the place in the ground where a dead person is buried.

I tried to think about Gatsby for a moment but he was already too far away. I could only remember without anger that Daisy hadn't sent a telegram or a flower.

As we walked down to the cars the man with the enormous round glasses said, "I couldn't get to the house."

"No one else could either," I said.

"My God! They used to go there by the hundreds—the poor son-of-a-bitch,"[1] he said.

One of the my most vivid memories is of coming back West from prep school[2] and later from college at Christmas time— coming back to our snow and our cold winters. I see now that this has been a story of the West after all—Tom and Gatsby, Daisy and Jordan and I were all westerners. And perhaps we possessed some deficiency in common which made us unadaptable to eastern life.

After Gatsby's death the East was no longer the place for me, and I decided to come back home.

There was one thing to be done before I left, because I wanted to leave things in order. I saw Jordan Baker and talked to her about what had happened to us. When I had finished she told me she was engaged to another man. We shook hands and I turned away and left.

One afternoon late in October I saw Tom Buchanan walking ahead of me on Fifth Avenue. Suddenly he saw me and walked back, holding out his hand.

---

1. **son-of-a-bitch** : (offensive word) a bad person, a bastard.
2. **prep school** : (in the USA) a private school that prepares pupils for college.

"What's the matter, Nick? Do you refuse to shake hands with me?"

"Yes. You know what I think of you. What did you tell Wilson that afternoon?"

He stared at me without a word and I knew that I had guessed correctly. I started to turn away but he took my arm. "I told him the truth," he said. "He came to the door while I was getting ready to leave. The butler said we weren't in but he forced his way upstairs. He was crazy enough to kill me if I hadn't told him who owned the car. His hand was on a gun in his pocket." He stopped suddenly. "What if I told him? Gatsby deserved it. He ran over Myrtle like a dog and he never even stopped the car."

There was nothing I could say. I couldn't tell him that Daisy was driving and not Gatsby.

"I suffered too, you know. When I went to close the flat and saw the box of dog food I sat down and cried like a baby. It was awful."

I couldn't forgive him or like him. But I saw that to him, what he had done was right. It was all very careless and confused. Tom and Daisy were careless people. They broke up things and creatures and then returned to their money or carelessness, or whatever it was that kept them together and let other people clean up the mess they had made.

I shook hands with him. It seemed silly not to, for I suddenly felt I was talking to a child.

Gatsby's house was still empty when I left. I spent my Saturday nights in New York because his parties were so alive in my memory that I could still hear the music and the laughter.

On the last night I went over and looked at the huge failure of a house once more. Then I went to sit on the beach. As I sat there I thought of Gatsby's wonder when he first saw the green light at the end of Daisy's dock.

His dream must have seemed so close that he could hardly fail to grasp [1] it. Gatsby believed in the green light, the enchanted future. He didn't know that as we move forward towards a dream, it moves further away from us. And so we go on, like boats sailing against the current, always taken back into the past.

---

1. **grasp** : (here) hold firmly.

The text and **beyond**

1 **Comprehension check**

Say whether the following sentences are True (T) or False (F), and then correct the false ones.

		T	F
1	The newspapers wrote accurate stories about Gatsby's death.	☐	☐
2	Gatsby's father did not show any emotion at his son's death.	☐	☐
3	Nick arranged Gatsby's funeral.	☐	☐
4	Meyer Wolfshiem was responsible for Gatsby's success.	☐	☐
5	Meyer Wolfshiem did not want to go to Gatsby's funeral.	☐	☐
6	Gatsby's father was proud of his son's great wealth.	☐	☐
7	Gatsby never paid any attention to his father.	☐	☐
8	Apart from Nick and Gatsby's father, only one person came to Gatsby's funeral.	☐	☐
9	Tom had told Wilson that Gatsby owned the car because he was afraid that Wilson would kill him.	☐	☐
10	In the end, Nick shook hands with Tom because he forgave him.	☐	☐

2 **Final events**

Talk about these moments in Chapter Ten. Did you find any of them surprising? Did you find any of them moving?

1 No one wanting to take care of Gatsby's funeral.
2 Wolshiem not wanting to attend the funeral.
3 The arrival of Gatsby's father.
4 Few people attending the funeral.
5 The arrival of the man with glasses at the funeral.
6 Nick not telling Tom that Daisy was driving.
7 Nick shaking Tom's hand.

Discussion topics

In pairs or small groups, choose a couple of the following discussion topics, or let your teacher choose. Then discuss them among yourselves, and report to the class.

1 The epigraph

An epigraph is a short quotation that an author puts at the beginning of a literary work to suggest its theme. Fitzgerald chose the lines below as the epigraph for *The Great Gatsby*. Why, do you think?

Then wear the gold hat, if that will move her; [1]
If you can bounce high, bounce for her too,
Till she cry, "Lover, gold-hatted, high-bouncing lover,
I must have you!"
Thomas Parke D'Invilliers

(Note: Thomas Parke D'Invilliers is both a pen name used by Fitzgerald himself and a character in his semi-autobiographical first novel, *This Side of Paradise*.)

2 Fitzgerald on story writing

F. Scott Fitzgerald wrote "What people are ashamed of usually makes a good story." How does this apply to Jay Gatsby?

3 "The American Dream"

"The American Dream" is the idea that in America any person, no matter how poor or disadvantaged, can, with hard work, become successful. The story of James Gatz and his transformation into the great Jay Gatsby is F. Scott Fitzgerald's description of what had happened to the American Dream in the 1920s.

1   How does Jay Gatsby's story show that the "American Dream" was still valid?

2   How does his story show that the "American Dream" had been corrupted?

1.   **move her** : make her feel romantic, tender emotions toward you.

4 The past

Nick says to Gatsby, "You can't **repeat the past**." Gatsby responds, "Why, of course you can!"

1　How does Gatsby try to repeat the past?
2　Whose opinion about the past is right, Gatsby's or Nick's?

5 A nice girl

1　What does Gatsby mean when he refers to Daisy as a "nice girl"?
2　How does Gatsby see Daisy?
3　How does Fitzgerald portray Daisy?
4　Why does Daisy hope that her daughter will grow up to be "a beautiful little fool"?

6 Honesty

1　Nick tells us that he is "one of the few honest people that I have ever known.". Describe the relationship of Tom, Daisy and Gatsby with the truth.
2　Does Nick remain an "honest person" during his long summer with the wealthy people of Long Island?

7 The hero

At the very end of the story Nick shouts to Gatsby, "They're a rotten crowd. You're worth the whole bunch of them!" He then adds, "I've always been glad I said that. It was the only compliment I ever gave him, because I disapproved of him from beginning to end."

1　Who is the "rotten crowd" that Nick is referring to?
2　Why does he think that Gatsby is "worth the whole bunch of them"?
3　Why has Nick disapproved of Gatsby "from beginning to end"?

8 Love

The Great Gatsby is also about love. Describe briefly the relationship between:

1　Tom and Daisy　　　　2　Daisy and Gatsby
3　Nick and Jordan Baker　4　Myrtle and George

▶▶▶ **INTERNET** PROJECT ◀◀◀

Connect to the Internet and go to www.blackcat-cideb.com or
www.cideb.it. Insert the title or part of the title of the book into our
search engine. Open the page for *The Great Gatsby*. Click on the
Internet project link. Go down the page until you find the title of this
book and click on the relevant link for this project.

- Apart from 'The Roaring Twenties' the1920s were also known as
  'The Jazz Age'. Read the article on jazz: what was the importance
  of jazz then, and how did people feel about it?
- In Fitzgerald's *The Great Gatsby* someone plays the song 'Ain't
  We Got Fun' at one of Gatsby's parties. Listen to this song in the
  audio gallery: what is the tone of the song? Read the words: are
  the singers rich or poor? Why do you think people say this song
  'captures the spirit of the twenties'?

Skyscrapers are one of the symbols of the American 1920s. And New York's Chrysler Building has architectural references to the automobile, the symbol of the machine age.

- Look through all the images of the Chrysler Building. Choose one that you like most, and explain why.
- Click on the link to Art Deco, a decorative style popular in the 1920s. What were the features of this style? Do you like it?

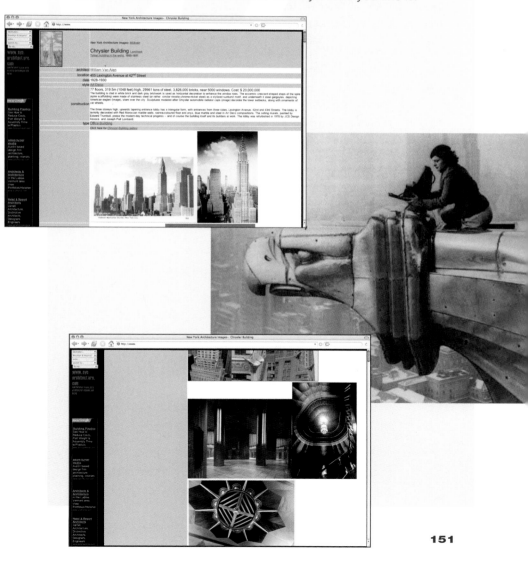

FCE ❶ Comprehension check

Choose the best answer — A, B, C or D — for the following questions.

1 What was Nick's father's advice to him?

   A ☐ Go into the bond business.

   B ☐ Don't criticize people because not everybody has had your advantages.

   C ☐ Rent a house in the country.

   D ☐ Go and live in New York.

2 What was across the bay from Nick's house?

   A ☐ East Egg, where his second cousin Daisy, lived

   B ☐ the fabulous mansion of Jay Gatsby

   C ☐ the more fashionable West Egg

   D ☐ New York City

3 When does the story take place?

   A ☐ during the summer of 1917

   B ☐ during the late summer and early fall of 1922

   C ☐ during the summer of 1922

   D ☐ during the summer of 1919

4 What does Daisy want her daughter to be when she grows up?

   A ☐ a professional golfer like her friend Jordan Baker

   B ☐ a beautiful little fool

   C ☐ a good wife

   D ☐ beautiful and wealthy

5 What was the story that Nick had heard about Jordan Baker?

   A ☐ that she had cheated during a golf tournament

   B ☐ that she was a friend of Jay Gatsby's

   C ☐ that she had been responsible for a terrible car accident

   D ☐ that she was a friend of Meyer Wolfshiem's

6 What was the amazing thing that Gatsby had told Jordan Baker?

   A ☐ that he wanted Nick to invite Daisy over to his house

   B ☐ that he had already met her in Louisville, Kentucky

C ☐ that he was still in love with Daisy

D ☐ that he wanted Daisy to tell Tom that she had never loved him

7 Why did Gatsby tell Nick about his life the first time?

A ☐ because he didn't want Nick to believe all the stories that people told about him

B ☐ because he didn't want Nick to think that he was a gangster

C ☐ because he had to ask Nick a favor

D ☐ because he wanted Nick to know about the sad thing that had happened to him a long time ago

8 Why didn't Nick accept Gatsby's offer?

A ☐ because he had enough work already

B ☐ because it was not the kind of job he knew how to do

C ☐ because he was afraid that he would have to work with some of Gatsby's criminal friends

D ☐ because he thought that Gatsby was offering him the job to repay a favor

9 Why did Daisy begin crying during her first meeting with Gatsby?

A ☐ because she realized that she had never loved Tom

B ☐ because she had never seen shirts as beautiful as the ones Gatsby had

C ☐ because she had never seen a house as magnificent as Gatsby's

D ☐ because she realized that Gatsby was the only real love of her life

10 When did James Gatz invent "the Great Gatsby"?

A ☐ after he became friends with Dan Cody

B ☐ after he became friends with Meyer Wolfshiem

C ☐ when he was still a teenager

D ☐ after he realized that he was too poor to marry Dais

153

11 How did Wilson discover that Gatsby owned the yellow car that had killed his wife?

A ☐ the police told him

B ☐ Tom told him

C ☐ the Greek, Michaelis, told him

D ☐ Jordan Baker told hi

12 Why didn't Meyer Wolfshiem go to Gatsby's funeral?

A ☐ because he only heard about Gatsby's death after the funeral was over

B ☐ because he was not particularly sad that Gatsby had died

C ☐ because his rule was to never get involved when somebody was killed

D ☐ because he was ashamed to be seen at the funeral of a person who had once been so poor

13 Why did Tom say that Gatsby deserved to die?

A ☐ because he thought that Gatsby was driving the car that had hit Myrtle

B ☐ because he was a bootlegger

C ☐ because he was not from a wealthy family

D ☐ because he had caused trouble in Tom's family

❷ Summary

Below is a summary of *The Great Gatsby*, but four paragraphs have been removed. Choose from paragraphs A-E the one which fits each gap. There is one extra paragraph which you do not need to use.

Nick Carraway, a young man from a well-to-do Midwestern family, went East to New York to learn about the bond business. He rented a small house on Long Island at a place called West Egg. Next door there was the mansion of a millionaire, Jay Gatsby. Across the bay from Nick's house was another town called East Egg, where Nick's wealthy second cousin, Daisy, lived with her husband, Tom Buchanan. Daisy invited Nick to visit. During the visit, Nick discovered that Tom had a mistress, a fact he didn't try to hide from Daisy. Nick also met Daisy's friend, Jordan Baker.

1 ....

One day a driver came to invite Nick to one of Gatsby's fabulous parties. Nick went to the party and by chance met Jordan Baker. Later Nick met a handsome, elegant young man, and the two men talked about their time in France during the war. Talking to him, Nick discovered that he was Jay Gatsby. Later Gatsby asked Jordan if he could speak to her alone. When Jordan returned she told Nick that Gatsby had told her something amazing, which she would tell him another time.

2 ....

Nick got home at two o'clock in the morning and Gatsby came over and began talking to Nick. He asked him when it would be best to invite Daisy. Nick suggested that she should come in a couple of days. Two days later it was raining, and Gatsby came over to wait for Daisy. Gatsby was extremely nervous because Daisy was a little late, but finally she arrived. The meeting between Daisy and Gatsby was very awkward at first but finally they began to relax. Gatsby then took Nick and Daisy to his house. Daisy was impressed. In the end, Nick left the two lovers alone.

3 ....

They decided to take out a suite at a hotel. Once in the suite, Tom confronted Gatsby with the situation. Gatsby told Tom that Daisy had never loved him, and he also told Daisy to tell Tom this. Tom accused Gatsby of being involved with criminals. Daisy was frightened by these accusations and it became clear that she had lost the courage she had once had to leave Tom. Tom told Daisy to drive home with Gatsby. A little later when Nick, Jordan and Tom arrived at George's gas station, they discovered that Myrtle had run out into the road and been killed by Gatsby's car. At the Buchanans' house Tom and Jordan went inside and Nick waited outside for a taxi. Gatsby walked up to him. They talked and Nick realized that it was Daisy who had hit Myrtle and that Gatsby was willing to accept the blame to defend Daisy.

4 ....

A In July Gatsby came to visit Nick for the first time. He invited Nick to come to the city with him and told him about himself and that Jordan had to tell him something. Later that day Nick went to the Plaza Hotel to have tea with Jordan and she told Nick about Daisy and Gatsby. Daisy, who came from a wealthy family, met Gatsby during the war. He was a handsome young soldier and they fell in love. But only a year later Gatsby went away to fight in France and Daisy met and married another man, Tom Buchanan. Jordan told Nick that Gatsby wanted him to invite Daisy to his house, but without telling her about Gatsby.

B   One Sunday Tom took Nick to meet his mistress. She lived with her husband, George Wilson, who ran a gas station. George did not suspect at all that Myrtle was Tom's mistress. That same day Tom, Nick and Myrtle went to New York to the apartment that Tom rented for Myrtle. They invited a few friends and they all drank a lot. The party ended when Myrtle began to repeat Daisy's name in order to tease Tom. Tom got angry and hit Myrtle, breaking her nose.

C   Nick couldn't sleep and early in the morning he went over to Gatsby's house. Gatsby told him how he had met Daisy and how he realized that he could never have such a rich girl because he was so poor. Daisy was the essence of all his dreams of success. Nick finally went to work. Gatsby decided to take a swim before the cold weather came. That afternoon George Wilson arrived. He had discovered that Gatsby was the owner of the yellow car that had killed his wife. He then killed Gatsby and took his own life. Nick arranged Gatsby's funeral, to which only three people came: Nick, Gatsby's father and one of the hundreds of people who had come to Gatsby's fabulous parties.

D   The parties were always magnificent and when Daisy came the first time she realized that she still loved Gatsby. The five years in which they had not seen each other seemed like nothing, and she started coming to his house, often with her daughter. Gatsby could not accept that the little girl was Daisy and Tom's daughter. The moment had come to confront Tom and Gatsby decided to organize a meeting at Nick's house.

E   One Saturday night many cars drove up to Gatsby's house for one of his usual parties, but that night there was no party. Gatsby did not need the parties to find Daisy. The next day Gatsby phoned Nick to invite him to Daisy's for lunch the following day. The day of the lunch was very hot and the situation was incredibly tense. Tom was talking to Myrtle's husband George on the phone about a car. George needed money because he wanted to take Myrtle West: he had discovered that Myrtle had a lover. Then it became obvious to Tom that Gatsby and Daisy were in love. Finally, they decided to drive into the city. Daisy went with Gatsby in Tom's car, and Nick and Jordan went with Tom in Gatsby's car.

3 Characters

Say which of the characters from *The Great Gatsby* is speaking. Choose from the characters in the box. There is one name you do not need to use.

> Jordan Baker   Daisy Buchanan   Tom Buchanan
> Nick Carraway   Nick Carraway's father   Dan Cody
> Jay Gatsby   Meyer Wolfshiem   Henry Gatz
> George Wilson   Myrtle Wilson

Example:

1   People think I am a dishonest man. This may be true, but I do appreciate my friends and I do help people realize their dreams. One in particular became wealthy and famous. Now, sadly, he is dead, and I certainly have cried, but for me, what we did for him while he was alive is more important than tears and flowers at a friend's graveside. And for this particular friend I did everything.

A   Meyer Wolfshiem ....

2   What on earth is the truth? What is honesty? I don't know and to tell you the truth (if I may use that word) I don't care. The main thing is to be happy, to win and to go where you want. Let the others be truthful. Let the others be careful! And love? Well, OK, if it is amusing. And if you are married and have a lover be very, very careful that your lover does not call you during dinner. That would be quite unforgivable!

B   ....

3   He provided me with some hope for my future. He provided me with a way out of my dreary, sad life of unending days in a squalid house in a gray desolate land. He conquered my heart, perhaps, but

certainly he satisfied my desires, physical and material. But in the end there was no escape and when I tried to run; death held me back.

C   ....

4   My family has been important for three generations ever since my father came to our Midwestern town back in 1851. He started a business which I still work in. But, despite all the advantages I have had in life and the advantages I have made sure that my son has had, I believe we should not judge people harshly. This is important, and I hope my son who is coming to maturity in this crazy Jazz Age will always remember this.

D   ....

5   Wealth! Wealth! I won it with cold, hard work. Yes, I did, and I deserved it too, even though many were more intelligent than me. But in the end, money brought me only whiskey and women, women who wanted only my money. But there was one smile that remains with me even in death. It is the smile of a poor, young man, and I wonder if that young man ever realized his dreams and if his dreams brought him more happiness than my dream brought me.

E   ....

6   What is love? What is the meaning of life? Is it having children? A man who loves you? A husband? Or is it simply having beautiful things? Beautiful cars? Beautiful shirts? Oh, it is all too difficult to understand, and today I am tired and the weather is hot. I will ask someone to explain it to me, maybe, but now I must go and change for dinner. At least dinner is real and tomorrow, maybe, if I am not too tired I will try to understand more.

F   ....

7   Who cares if I lived most of my life in poverty! In the end I saw that in me was something great, something that could produce great wealth, that could make this great country grow. Yes, indeed, and as I walked around that magnificent mansion and admired its marble, silver and gold, I knew that something in my own miserable life could make this dream come true.

G   ....

8 They will destroy us in the end! I am sure of it! The dark races! The nouveau riche! The gangsters! The criminals! I know this and my own sad, sad experience is proof. In my own life, one of these criminals even tried to steal my dear, dear wife, and in the process even killed my girl... I mean, a friend of mine. This is the truth, which only the strong and noble of America's true aristocracy can know, and I— thank God!—am one of them!

H ....

9 They both thought I was stupid and maybe they were right. But in the end they paid! God, who is watching us all day and night, even in this desolate gray land, saw his crimes and he paid for it! But still, why didn't God let us go West and start over again! I am sure we could have been happy.

I ....

10 A man with a splendid smile capable of true love who is a criminal, and a man with a horrible smile incapable of love. A lovely young woman of a charm and talent who cares nothing for morals. A fragile young, careless mother in love with the surface splendor of life. What can I say about them? I can say what I saw but I don't wish to judge them; after all, not everybody has been as lucky as I have!

j ....

Key to the Exit Test

1 **1**B; **2**A; **3**C; **4**B; **5**A; **6**A; **7**A; **8**D; **9**A; **10**C; **11**B; **12**C; **13**A

2 **1**B; **2**A; **3**E; **4**C

3 **B** Jordan Baker; **C** Myrtle Wilson; **D** Nick Carraway's father; **E** Dan Cody; **F** Daisy Buchanan; **G** Henry Gatz; **H** Tom Buchanan; **I** George Wilson; **J** Nick Carraway

This reader uses the **EXPANSIVE READING** approach, where the text becomes a springboard to improve language skills and to explore historical background, cultural connections and other topics suggested by the text.

The new structures introduced in this step of our **READING & TRAINING** series are listed below. Naturally, structures from lower steps are included too. For a complete list of structures used over all the six steps, see *The Black Cat Guide to Graded Readers*, which is also downloadable at no cost from our website, blackcat-cideb.com.

The vocabulary used at each step is carefully checked against vocabulary lists used for internationally recognised examinations.

Step **Five** B2.2

All the structures used in the previous levels, plus the following:

Verb tenses
Present Perfect and Past Perfect Simple:
  negative duration *(haven't ... for ages)*
Present Perfect Continuous: recent activities
  leading to present situation
Past Perfect Continuous

Verb forms and patterns
Passive forms: Past Perfect Simple;
  with modal verbs
Reported speech introduced by more examples
  of precise reporting verbs (e.g. *threaten,
  insist, complain*)
Wish and *if only* + past tense
It's time + past tense

Modal verbs
Should(n't) have, ought (not) to have:
  duty in the past
*Must have, can't have, may have, might have,
  could have*: deduction and probability in
  the past

Types of clause
3rd conditionals with *unless*
Mixed conditional sentences
Complex sentences with more than one
  subordinate clause